THE MOUNTAIN IS YOU

TRANSFORMING SELF-SABOTAGE INTO SELF-MASTERY

BRIANNA WIEST

THOUGHT CATALOG Books

THOUGHTCATALOG.COM
NEW YORK · LOS ANGELES

THOUGHT
CATALOG
Books

Published by Thought Catalog Books, an imprint of the digital magazine Thought Catalog, which is owned and operated by The Thought & Expression Company LLC, an independent media organization based in Brooklyn, New York and Los Angeles, California.

This book was produced by Chris Lavergne and Noelle Beams and designed by KJ Parish. Visit us on the web at thoughtcatalog.com and shopcatalog.com.

Made in the United States of America.

ISBN 978-1-949759-22-8

10 9 8 7 6 5 4 3 2 1

"Brianna's book is a beautiful expression of healing. Her insights on self-sabotage, emotional intelligence, and deep transformation are invaluable. She understands that change begins with self, and her book is a gift to the collective."

– DR. NICOLE LEPERA, *"The Holistic Psychologist"*

"I'm of the belief that in fulfilling our deepest potential, the greatest rewards come less from outcomes and more from who we must become in order to achieve what we know we are truly capable of. In this beautifully written and eye-opening book, Brianna Wiest inspires us to scale our own mountains with powerful insights to help prepare you for the climb ahead. A must-read for those ready to do the inner work required to live a life of fulfillment, wonder, and enjoyment!"

– SIMON ALEXANDER ONG, *International Life Coach & Business Strategist*

"*The Mountain Is You* is a wake-up call that inspires hope in adversity. You're invited to burn the rules of what you've been taught about yourself, as you awaken your inner hero and consciously choose a new narrative, and ultimately, create a life you deeply desire and deserve. Brianna provides an alchemy of pragmatic tools and deep soul shifts to build the courage and clarity required to climb your own personal mountain—and essentially, remember who you came here to be. The ultimate seeker's guide for those brave enough to face their true north and take their power back."

– JENNA BLACK, *International Coach*

"Brianna Wiest is one of my favorite writers. She combines life-changing wisdom with a unique eloquence that inspires readers to reclaim their power and change their lives for the better. *The Mountain Is You* is bound to help many people."

– YUNG PUEBLO, *Best-Selling Author of "Inward"*

"A revelation. The words wrote struck me so deep inside, there were several moments that I had to pause from reading because my eyes filled with tears of realization and confirmation."

– DAWN ZULUETA, *Film-Television Actress, Host & Model*

"Brianna Wiest's masterpiece is the perfect roadmap for understanding why we self-sabotage, when we do it, and how to stop doing it—for good."

– DR. STEVEN EISENBERG, *Wellbeing & Connection Expert, Renowned Internist & Oncologist*

INTRODUCTION

MUCH LIKE NATURE, life is very often working in our favor, even when it seems like we are only being faced with adversity, discomfort, and change.

As forest fires are essential to the ecology of the environment—opening new seeds that require heat to sprout and rebuild a population of trees—our minds also go through periodic episodes of positive disintegration, or a cleansing through which we release and renew our self-concept. We know that nature is most fertile and expansive at its perimeters, where climates meet, and we also transform when we reach our edge states, the points at which we are forced to step out of our comfort zones and regroup.[1] When we can no longer rely on our coping mechanisms to help distract us from the problems in our lives, it can feel as though we've hit rock bottom. The reality is that this sort of awakening is what happens when we finally come to terms with the problems that have existed for a long time. The breakdown is often just the tipping point that precedes the breakthrough, the moment a star implodes before it becomes a supernova.

Just as a mountain is formed when two sections of the ground are forced against one another, your mountain will arise out of coexisting but conflicting needs. Your mountain requires you to reconcile two parts of you: the conscious and the unconscious, the part of you that is aware of what you want and the part of you that is not aware of why you are still holding yourself back.

Historically, mountains have been used as metaphors for spiritual awakenings, journeys of personal growth, and of course, insurmountable challenges that seem impossible to overcome when we are standing at the bottom. Like so much of nature, mountains provide us with an inherent wisdom about what it will take to rise up to our highest potential.

The objective of being human is to grow. We see this reflected back to us in every part of life. Species reproduce, DNA evolves to eliminate certain strands and develop new ones, and the edges of the universe are expanding forever outward. Likewise, our ability to feel the depth and beauty of life is capable of expanding forever inward if we are willing to take our problems and see them as catalysts. Forests need fire to do this, volcanoes need implosions, stars need collapse, and human beings often need to be faced with no other option but to change before they really do.

To have a mountain in front of you does not mean you are fundamentally broken in some way. Everything in nature is imperfect, and it is because of that imperfection that growth is possible. If everything existed in uniformity, the gravity that created the stars and planets and everything that we know would not exist. Without breaks, faults, and gaps, nothing could grow and nothing would become.[2] The fact that you are imperfect is not a sign that you have failed; it is a sign that you are human, and more importantly, it is a sign that you still have more potential within you.

Maybe you know what your mountain is. Maybe it's addiction, weight, relationships, jobs, motivation, or money. Maybe you don't. Maybe it's a vague sense of anxiety, low self-esteem, fear, or a general discontentment that seems to bleed out onto everything else. The mountain is often less a challenge in front of us as it is a problem within us, an unstable foundation that might not seem evident on the surface but is nonetheless shifting almost every part of our lives.

Usually when we have a problem that is circumstantial, we are facing the reality of life. When we have a problem that is chronic, we are facing the reality of ourselves. We often think that to face a mountain means to face life's hardships, but the truth is that it is almost always because of the years we have spent accumulating tiny traumas, adaptations, and coping mechanisms, all of which have compounded over time.

> Your mountain is the block between you and the life you want to live. Facing it is also the only path to your freedom and becoming. You are here because a trigger showed you to your wound, and your wound will show you to your path, and your path will show you to your destiny.

When you arrive at this breaking point—the foot of the mountain, the heat of the fire, the night that finally wakes you—you are at the crux of the breakdown, and if you are willing to do the work, you will find that it is the entryway to the breakthrough you have spent your entire life waiting for.

Your old self can no longer sustain the life you are trying to lead; it is time for reinvention and rebirth.

You must release your old self into the fire of your vision and be willing to think in a way you have never even tried before. You must mourn the loss of your younger self, the person who has gotten you this far but who is no longer equipped to carry you onward. You must envision and become one with your future self, the hero of your life that is going to lead you from here. The task in front of you is silent, simple, and monumental. It is a feat most do not ever get to the point of attempting. You must now learn agility, resilience, and self-understanding. You must change completely, never to be the same again.

The mountain that stands in front of you is the calling of your life, your purpose for being here, and your path finally made clear. One day, this mountain will be behind you, but who you become in the process of getting over it will stay with you always.

In the end, it is not the mountain that you must master, but yourself.

CHAPTER 1

THE MOUNTAIN IS YOU

THERE IS NOTHING HOLDING you back in life more than yourself.

If there is an ongoing gap between where you are and where you want to be—and your efforts to close it are consistently met with your own resistance, pain, and discomfort—self-sabotage is almost always at work.

On the surface, self-sabotage seems masochistic. It appears to be a product of self-hatred, low confidence, or a lack of willpower. In reality, self-sabotage is simply the presence of an unconscious need that is being fulfilled by the self-sabotaging behavior. To overcome this, we must go through a process of deep psychological excavation. We must pinpoint the traumatic event, release unprocessed emotions, find healthier ways to meet our needs, reinvent our self-image, and develop principles such as emotional intelligence and resilience.

It is no small task, and yet it is the work that all of us must do at one point or another.

SELF-SABOTAGE IS NOT ALWAYS OBVIOUS AT THE ONSET

When Carl Jung was a child, he fell on the ground in school and hit his head. When he got hurt, he thought to himself: "Yes, maybe I won't have to go back to school now."[3]

Though he is known today for his insightful body of work, he actually didn't like school or fit in well with his peers. Shortly after his accident, Jung began experiencing sporadic and uncontrollable fainting spells. He unconsciously developed what he would call a "neurosis" and ultimately came to realize that all neuroses are "substitute[s] for legitimate suffering."

In Jung's case, he made an unconscious association between fainting and getting out of school. He came to believe that the fainting spells were a manifestation of his unconscious desire to get out of class, where he felt uncomfortable and unhappy. Likewise, for many people, their fears and attachments are very often just symptoms of deeper issues for which they do not have any better way to cope.

·

SELF-SABOTAGE IS A COPING MECHANISM

Self-sabotage is what happens when we refuse to consciously meet our innermost needs, often because we do not believe we are capable of handling them.

Sometimes, we sabotage our relationships because what we really want is to find ourselves, though we are afraid to be alone. Sometimes, we sabotage our professional success because what we really want is to create art, even if it will make us seem less ambitious by society's measures. Sometimes, we sabotage our healing journey by psychoanalyzing our feelings, because doing so ensures we avoid actually experiencing them. Sometimes, we sabotage our self-talk because if we believed in ourselves, we'd feel free to get back out in the world and take risks, and that would leave us vulnerable.

In the end, self-sabotage is very often just a maladaptive coping mechanism, a way we give ourselves what we need without having to actually address what that need is. But like any coping mechanism, it is just that — a way to cope. It's not an answer, it's not a solution, and it does not ever truly solve the problem. We are merely numbing our desires, and giving ourselves a little taste of temporary relief.

SELF-SABOTAGE COMES FROM IRRATIONAL FEAR

Sometimes, our most sabotaging behaviors are really the result of long-held and unexamined fears we have about the world and ourselves.

Perhaps it is the idea that you are unintelligent, unattractive, or disliked. Perhaps it is the idea of losing a job, taking an elevator, or committing to a relationship. In other cases, it can be more abstract, such as the concept of someone "coming to get" you, violating your boundaries, getting "caught," or being wrongly accused.

These beliefs become attachments over time.

For most people, the abstract fear is really a representation of a legitimate fear. Because it would be too scary to actually dwell on the real fear, we project those feelings onto issues or circumstances that are less likely to occur. If the situation has an extremely low likelihood of becoming reality, it therefore becomes a "safe" thing to worry about, because subconsciously, we already know it isn't going to happen. Therefore, we have an avenue to express our feelings without actually endangering ourselves.

For example, if you are someone who is deeply afraid of being a passenger in a car, maybe your real fear is the loss of control or the idea that someone or something else is controlling your life. Perhaps the fear is of "moving forward," and the moving car is simply a representation of that.

If you were aware of the real issue, you could begin working to resolve it, perhaps by identifying the ways you are giving up your power or being too passive. However, if you aren't aware of the real problem, you'll continue to spend your time trying to convince yourself to not be triggered and anxious while riding in the car and find that it only gets worse.

If you try to fix the problem on the surface, you will always come up against a wall. This is because you're trying to rip off a Band-Aid before you have a strategy to heal the wound.

SELF-SABOTAGE COMES FROM UNCONSCIOUS, NEGATIVE ASSOCIATIONS

Self-sabotage is also one of the first signs that your inner narrative is outdated, limiting, or simply incorrect.

Your life is defined not only by what you think about it, but also what you think of yourself. Your self-concept is an idea that you have spent your whole life building. It was created by piecing together inputs and influences from those around you: what your parents believed, what your peers thought, what became self-evident through personal experience, and so on. Your self-image is difficult to adjust, because your brain's confirmation bias works to affirm your preexisting beliefs about yourself.

When we self-sabotage, it is often because we have a negative association between achieving the goal we aspire to and being the kind of person who has or does that thing.

If your issue is that you want to be financially stable, and yet you keep ruining every effort you make to get there, you have to go back to your first concept of money. How did your parents manage their finances? More importantly, what did they tell you about people who had it and people who didn't? Many people who struggle financially will justify their place in life by disavowing money as a whole. They will say that all rich people are terrible. If you grew up with people who told you your entire life that people who have money are this way, guess what you're going to resist having?

Your anxiety around the issue that you're self-sabotaging is usually a reflection of your limiting belief.

Maybe you associate being healthy with being vulnerable, because you had a parent who was perfectly healthy when they suddenly fell ill. Maybe you aren't writing your magnum opus because you don't really want to write; you just want to be seen as "successful" because that will get you praise, which is typically what people revert to when they want acceptance but haven't gotten it. Maybe you keep eating the wrong foods because they soothe you, but you haven't stopped to ask what they have to keep soothing you *from*. Maybe you aren't really a pessimist but don't know how to connect with the people in your life other than by complaining to them.

In order to reconcile this, you have to begin to challenge these preexisting ideas and then adopt new ones.

You have to be able to recognize that not everybody with money is corrupt, not by a long shot. Even more importantly, given that there *are* people who use their money in selfish ways, it is even more important that good people with great intentions are fearless in pursuit of acquiring this essential tool to create more time, opportunity, and wellness for themselves and others. You have to recognize that being healthy makes you less vulnerable, not more, and that criticism comes with creating anything for the public and isn't a reason to *not* do it. You have to show yourself that there are many different ways to self-soothe that are more effective than unhealthy food choices and that there are far better ways to connect with others than through negativity.

Once you begin to really question and observe these pre-existing beliefs, you begin to see how warped and illogical they were all along—not to mention distinctly holding you back from your ultimate potential.

SELF-SABOTAGE COMES FROM WHAT'S UNFAMILIAR

Human beings experience a natural resistance to the unknown, because it is essentially the ultimate loss of control. This is true even if what's "unknown" is benevolent or even beneficial to us.

Self-sabotage is very often the simple product of unfamiliarity, and it is because anything that is foreign, no matter how good, will also be uncomfortable until it is also familiar. This often leads people to confuse the discomfort of the unknown with being "wrong" or "bad" or "ominous." However, it is simply a matter of psychological adjustment.

Gay Hendricks calls this your "upper limit," or your tolerance for happiness.[4] Everyone has a capacity for which they allow themselves to feel good. This is similar to what other psychologists refer to as a person's "baseline," or their set predisposition that they eventually revert back to, even if certain events or circumstances shift temporarily.

Small shifts, compounded over time, can result in permanent baseline adjustments. However, they often don't stick because we come up on our upper limits. The reason we don't allow those shifts to become baselines is because as soon as our circumstances extend beyond the amount of happiness we're accustomed to, we find ways both conscious and unconscious to bring ourselves back to a feeling we're comfortable with.

We are programmed to seek what we've known. Even though we think we're after happiness, we're actually trying to find whatever we're most used to.

SELF-SABOTAGE COMES FROM BELIEF SYSTEMS

What you believe about your life is what you will make true about your life.

That's why it's so crucial to be aware of these outdated narratives and have the courage to change them.

Maybe you have gone through the majority of your life believing that a standard $50K per year salary at a decent company is the most you'll ever be capable of. Maybe you've spent so many years telling yourself: "I am an anxious person," you started to actually identify with it, adopting anxiety and fear into your belief system about who you fundamentally are. Maybe you were raised in a closed-minded social circle or an echo chamber. Maybe you did not know that you could question or arrive at new conclusions about politics or religion. Maybe you never thought you were someone who could have great style, feel content, or travel the world.

In other cases, your limiting beliefs might come from wanting to keep yourself safe.

Maybe that's why you prefer the comfort of what you've known to the vulnerability of what you don't, why you prefer apathy to excitement, think that suffering makes you more worthy, or believe that for every good thing in life, there must also be an accompanying "bad."

To truly heal, you are going to have to change the way you think. You are going to have to become very conscious of negative and false beliefs and start shifting to a mindset that actually serves you.

HOW TO GET OUT OF DENIAL

Maybe this preliminary information about self-sabotage resonates a bit, or maybe it resonates a lot.

Either way, if you are here because you truly want to change your life, you are going to have to stop being in denial about your personal state of affairs. You are going to have to get real with yourself. You are going to have to decide that you love yourself too much to stop settling for less than what you really deserve.

If you think that you could be doing better in life, you might be right.

If you think that there is more that you are here to accomplish, you might be right.

If you think that you are not being your authentic self, you might be right.

It does not serve us to use endless affirmations to placate our true feelings about where we are in our journey. When we do this, we start dissociating and get stuck.

In an effort to "love ourselves," we try to validate everything about who we are. Yet those warm sentiments never quite seem to stick, only ever temporarily numbing the discomfort. Why don't they work? Because deep down, we know we are not quite being who we want to be, and until we accept this, we are never going to find peace.

When we are in denial, we tend to go into "blame" mode. We look for anyone or anything to explain why we are the way we are. Then we start justifying. If you have to constantly—on a near daily basis—rationalize why you're unhappy about your life, you are not doing yourself any favors. You are not getting any closer to creating the lasting change that you so deeply desire.

The first step in healing anything is taking full accountability. It is no longer being in denial about the honest truth of your life and yourself. It does not matter what your life looks like on the outside; it is how you feel about it on the inside. It is not okay to be constantly stressed, panicked, and unhappy. Something is wrong, and the longer you try to "love yourself" out of realizing this, the longer you are going to suffer.

> The greatest act of self-love is to no longer accept a life you are unhappy with. It is to be able to state the problem plainly and in a straightforward manner.

That is precisely what you need to do to continue truly uprooting your life and transforming it. It is the first step towards real change.

Take a piece of paper and a pen, and write down everything you aren't happy with. Write down, very specifically, every single problem you face. If you are struggling with finances, you need a very clear picture of what's wrong. Write down every debt, every bill, every asset, and every bit of income. If you are struggling with self-image, write down exactly what you dislike about yourself. If it is anxiety, write down everything that bothers or upsets you.

You must first and foremost get out of denial and into clarity about what's really wrong. At this point, you have a choice: You can make peace, or you can commit to changing. The lingering is what is keeping you stuck.

THE PATH BEGINS RIGHT WHERE YOU ARE NOW

If you know that change needs to be made in your life, it is okay if you are far away from your goal or if you cannot yet conceive how you will arrive.

It is okay if you are starting at the beginning.

It is okay if you are at rock bottom and cannot yet see your way through.

It is okay if you are at the foot of your mountain and have failed every time you've tried to overcome it.

Rock bottom is very often where we begin on our healing journey. This is not because we suddenly see the light, not because our worst days are magically transmuted into some type of epiphany, and not because someone saves us from our own madness. Rock bottom becomes a turning point because it is only at that point that most people think: *I never want to feel this way again.*

That thought is not just an idea. It is a declaration and a resolution. It is one of the most life-changing things you can ever experience. It becomes the foundation upon which you build everything else.

When you decide you truly do not ever want to feel a certain way again, you set out on a journey of self-awareness, learning, and growth that has you radically reinvent who you are.

In that moment, fault becomes irrelevant. You're no longer mulling over who did what or how you've been wronged. In that moment, only one thing guides you, and it is this: No matter what it takes, *I will never accept my life getting to this point again.*

Rock bottom isn't a bad day. It doesn't happen by chance. We only arrive at rock bottom when our habits begin to compound upon one another, when our coping mechanisms have spiraled so out of control that we can no longer resist the feelings we were attempting to hide. Rock bottom is when we are finally faced with ourselves, when everything has gone so wrong, we are left to realize that there is only one common denominator through it all.

We must heal. We must change. We must choose to turn around so that we will never feel this way again.

When we have a down day, we don't think: *I never want to feel this way again.* Why? Because it is not fun, but it's also not unbearable. Mostly, though, we are somewhat aware that small failures are a regular part of life; we are imperfect but trying our best, and that vague discomfort will pass eventually.

We don't reach a breaking point because one or two things go wrong. We reach a breaking point when we finally accept that the problem isn't how the world is; it is how we are. This is a beautiful reckoning to have. Ayodeji Awosika describes his own like this: "You must find the purest, purest, purest form of being fed up. Make it hurt. I literally screamed, 'I'm not going to fucking live like this anymore!'"

> Human beings are guided by comfort. They stay close to what feels familiar and reject what doesn't, even if it's objectively better for them.

Be this as it is, most people do not actually change their lives until not changing becomes the less comfortable option. This means that they do not actually embrace the difficulty of altering their habits until they simply do not have another choice. Staying where they are is not viable. They can no longer even pretend that it is desirable in any way. They are, quite honestly, less at rock bottom and more stuck between a rock that's impinging on them and an arduous climb out from beneath it.

If you really want to change your life, let yourself be consumed with rage: not toward others, not with the world, but within yourself.

Get angry, determined, and allow yourself to develop tunnel vision with one thing and one thing only at the end: that you will not go on as you are.

PREPARING FOR RADICAL CHANGE

One of the biggest reasons that people avoid doing important internal work is that they recognize if they heal themselves, their lives will change—sometimes drastically. If they come to terms with how unhappy they are, it means that they will have to temporarily be *more* uncomfortable, ashamed, or scared while they start all over.

Let's be clear about something: To put an end to your self-sabotaging behavior absolutely means that change is on the horizon.

Your new life is going to cost you your old one.

It's going to cost you your comfort zone and your sense of direction.

It's going to cost you relationships and friends.

It's going to cost you being liked and understood.

It doesn't matter.

The people who are meant for you are going to meet you on the other side. You're going to build a new comfort zone around the things that actually move you forward. Instead of being liked, you're going to be loved. Instead of being understood, you're going to be seen.

All you're going to lose is what was built for a person you no longer are.

Remaining attached to your old life is the first and final act of self-sabotage, and releasing it is what we must prepare for to truly be willing to see real change.

CHAPTER 2

THERE'S NO SUCH THING AS SELF-SABOTAGE

WHEN YOU HABITUATE YOURSELF to do things that move your life forward, you call them skills. When they hold your life back, you call them self-sabotage. They are both essentially the same function.

Sometimes, it happens by accident. Sometimes, we just get used to living a certain way and fail to have a vision for how life could be different. Sometimes, we make choices because we don't know how to make better ones or that anything else is even possible. Sometimes, we settle for what we're handed because we don't know we can ask for more. Sometimes, we run our lives on autopilot for long enough that we begin to think we no longer have a choice.

However, most of the time, it's not accidental at all. The habits and behaviors you can't stop engaging in—no matter how destructive or limiting they may be—are intelligently designed by your subconscious to meet an unfulfilled need, displaced emotion, or neglected desire.

> Overcoming self-sabotage is not about trying to figure out how to override your impulses; it is first determining why those impulses exist in the first place.

Self-sabotage is often misunderstood to be a way in which we punish, deride, or intentionally hurt ourselves. On the surface, this seems true enough. Self-sabotage is committing to a healthier diet and finding yourself pulling up to the drive-thru a few hours later. It's identifying a market gap, conceiving an unprecedentedly brilliant business idea, then getting "distracted" and forgetting to begin working on it. It's having strange and terrifying thoughts and allowing them to paralyze you in the face of important life changes or milestones. It is knowing you have so much to be grateful for and excited about and yet worrying anyway.

We often misattribute these behaviors to a lack of intelligence, willpower, or capability. That is usually not the case. Self-sabotage is not a way we hurt ourselves; it's a way we try to protect ourselves.

WHAT IS SELF-SABOTAGE?

Self-sabotage is when you have two conflicting desires. One is conscious, one is unconscious. You know how you want to move your life forward, and yet you are still, for some reason, stuck.

When you have big, ongoing, insurmountable issues in your life—especially when the solutions seem so simple, so easy, and yet so impossible to stick with—what you have are not big problems but big attachments.

People are pretty incredible in the fact that they basically do whatever they want to do.

This is true of everything in human life. Regardless of the potential consequences, human nature has revealed itself to be incredibly self-serving. People have an almost superhuman way of doing whatever they feel compelled to do, regardless of whom it could hurt, what wars it could spawn, or what future would be put at risk. When you consider this, you begin to realize that if you're keeping something in your life, there has to be a reason you want it there. The only question is why.

Some people can't figure out why they can't seem to motivate themselves enough to create a new business to facilitate their goal of becoming significantly wealthier, perhaps not realizing that they have a subconscious belief that to be rich is to be egocentric or disliked. Or perhaps they actually don't want to be super-wealthy. Maybe it's a cover-up for wanting to feel secure and "taken care of," or their real desire is to be recognized for their art, and as this feels too unlikely to ever happen, they fall back on a secondary dream that doesn't actually motivate them.

Some people say that they want to be successful at any

cost and yet don't want to log the hours of work it would take to get there. Perhaps it is because they understand at some level that being "successful" doesn't really make you happy nor liked. In fact, the opposite tends to be true. Success usually exposes you to jealousy and scrutiny. Successful people are not loved in the way that we imagine they would be; they are usually picked apart because envious people need to humanize them in some way. Perhaps instead of being "successful," what many really want is just to be loved, and yet their ambition for success directly threatens that.

Some people can't figure out why they keep choosing the "wrong" relationships, people whose patterns of rejection, abuse, or refusal to commit seem to be consistent. Perhaps they don't realize that they are actually re-creating the relationship dynamics they experienced when they were young because they associate love with loss or abandonment. Perhaps they want to re-create family relationships in which they felt helpless, but to live them again as an adult where they *can* help the addict, the liar, or the broken person.

When it comes to self-sabotaging behaviors, you have to understand that sometimes, it's easy to get attached to having problems.

Being successful can make you less liked.

Finding love can make you more vulnerable.

Making yourself less attractive can guard you.

Playing small allows you to avoid scrutiny.

Procrastinating puts you back in a place of comfort.

All the ways in which you are self-sabotaging are actually ways that you are feeding a need you probably do not even realize you have. Overcoming it is not only a matter of learning to understand yourself better, but realizing that your problems are not problems; they are symptoms.

You cannot get rid of the coping mechanisms and think you've solved the problem.

WHAT DOES SELF-SABOTAGE LOOK LIKE?

It's impossible to say decisively what self-sabotage does or doesn't look like, because certain habits and behaviors that can be healthy for one person can be unhealthy in another context.

With that said, there are definitely some specific behaviors and patterns that are typically indicative of self-sabotage, and they usually relate to being aware that there's a problem in your life, yet feeling the need to perpetuate it regardless. Here are some of the main signs that you're probably in a cycle of self-sabotage.

RESISTANCE

Resistance is what happens when we have a new project that we need to work on and simply can't bring ourselves to do it. It's when we get into a great new relationship and then keep bailing on plans. It's when we get an amazing idea for our business and then feel tension and anger when it comes time to sit down and actually get to work.

We often feel resistance in the face of what's going *right* in our lives, not what's going wrong. When we have a problem to solve, resistance is usually nowhere to be found. But when we have something to enjoy, create, or build, we are tapping into a part of ourselves that is trying to thrive instead of just survive, and the unfamiliarity can be daunting.

HOW TO RESOLVE THIS

Resistance is your way of slowing down and making sure that it's safe to get attached to something new and important. In other cases, it can also be a warning sign that something isn't quite right, and you might need to step back and regroup.

Resistance is not the same thing as procrastination or indifference and shouldn't be treated as such. When we are experiencing resistance, there is always a reason, and we have to pay attention. If we try to force ourselves to perform in the face of resistance, it usually intensifies the feeling, as we are strengthening the internal conflict and triggering the fear that's holding us back in the first place.

Instead, releasing resistance requires us to refocus. We have to get clear on what we want as well as when and why we want it. We have to identify unconscious beliefs that are preventing us from showing up, and then we have to step back into the work when we feel inspired. Wanting is the entryway to showing up after resistance.

HITTING YOUR UPPER LIMIT

As discussed before, there is only a certain amount of happiness that most of us will allow ourselves to feel. Gay Hendricks calls this your "upper limit."

Your upper limit is essentially the amount of "good" that you're comfortable having in your life. It is your tolerance and threshold for having positive feelings or experiencing positive events.

When you begin to surpass your upper limit, you start to unconsciously sabotage what's happening in order to bring yourself back to what's comfortable and familiar. For some people, this manifests physically, often as aches, pains, headaches, or physical tension. For others, it manifests emotionally as resistance, anger, guilt, or fear.

It might seem totally counterintuitive, but we are not

really wired to be happy; we are wired to be comfortable, and anything that is outside of that realm of comfort feels threatening or scary until we are familiar with it.

HOW TO RESOLVE THIS

Hitting your upper limit is a really great sign. It means that you're approaching and surpassing new levels of your life, and that is first and foremost something to congratulate yourself for. The way you resolve an upper-limit problem is by slowly acclimating yourself to your new "normal."

Instead of shocking yourself into big changes, allow yourself to slowly adjust and adapt. By taking it slow, you are allowing yourself to gradually reinstate a new comfort zone around what you want your life to be. Over time, you gradually shift your baseline to a new standard.

UPROOTING

Uprooting happens when someone finds themselves jumping from relationship to relationship or changing their business website again and again, when they really need to focus on confronting relationship issues when they arise or taking care of clients they already have. In uprooting, you are not allowing yourself to blossom; you are only comfortable with the process of sprouting.

It might be constantly needing a "fresh start," which is often the result of not having healthy ways to deal with stress or struggling with conflict resolution. Uprooting can be a way of diverting attention from the actual problems in your life, as your attention must go toward reestablishing oneself at a new job or in a new town.

Ultimately, uprooting means you are always just beginning your new chapter but never really finishing it. Despite your efforts to keep moving on, you end up more stuck than ever before.

HOW TO RESOLVE THIS

First, recognize the pattern.

One of the primary symptoms of uprooting is not realizing that one is doing it. Therefore, the most important step is to become aware of what's happening. Trace back your steps over the past few years: How many places have you moved or worked? Then figure out what is driving you away from each new thing you find.

Next, you need to get clear on what you really want. Sometimes, uprooting occurs because we step too quickly toward what we think we want, only to find that we didn't think it through and don't really want that thing very much. Clarity is key, because you're thinking long-term now. What would it look like to choose one place to live, then build connections there? What would it look like to work at the same place and move up in your position or build your business?

Remember that healing from an uprooting pattern is not about settling for something you don't want, nor is it about staying in an unsafe or unhealthy situation because you don't want to move again. It's about getting clear and determined on what's the right path for you and then making a plan for how you can thrive, not just survive. When the moment comes that you would typically flee, confront the discomfort and stay where you are. Figure out *why* you are uncomfortable getting attached to one thing or another, and determine what a healthy attachment would look like for you.

PERFECTIONISM

When we expect that our work must be perfect the first time we do it, we end up getting into a cycle of perfectionism.

Perfectionism isn't actually wanting everything to be right. It's not a good thing. In fact, it is a hindering thing, because it sets up unrealistic expectations about what we are capable of or what the outcomes of our lives could be.

Perfectionism holds us back from showing up and trying, or really doing the important work of our lives. This happens because when we are afraid of failing, or feeling vulnerable, or not being as good as we want others to think we are, we end up avoiding the work that is required to actually become that good. We sabotage ourselves because it is the willingness to show up and simply *do it,* again and again and again, that ultimately brings us to a place of mastery.

HOW TO RESOLVE THIS

Don't worry about doing it well; just do it.

Don't worry about writing a bestseller, just write. Don't worry about making a Grammy-winning hit, just make music. Don't worry about failing, just keep showing up and trying. At first, all that matters is that you *do* what you really want to do. From there, you can learn from your mistakes and over time get to the place where you really want to be.

The truth is that we actually do not accomplish great feats when we are anxious about whether or not what we do will indeed be something impressive and world-changing. We accomplish these sorts of things when we simply show up and allow ourselves to create something meaningful and important to us.

Instead of perfection, focus on progress. Instead of having something done perfectly, focus on just getting it done. From there, you can edit, build, grow, and develop it to exactly what your vision is. But if you don't get started, you'll never arrive.

LIMITED EMOTIONAL PROCESSING SKILLS

In life, there are going to be people, situations, and circumstances that are upsetting, infuriating, saddening, and even enraging. There will likewise be people, situations, and circumstances that are inspiring, hopeful, helpful, and truly offer purpose and meaning in your life.

When you are only able to process half of your emotions, you stunt yourself. You start going out of your way to avoid any possible situation that could bring up something frustrating or uncomfortable, because you have no tools to be able to handle that feeling. This means that you start avoiding the very risks and actions that would ultimately change your life for the better.

In addition, an inability to process your emotions means you get stuck with them. You sit and dwell on your anger and sadness because you don't know how to make them go away. When we can only process half of our emotions, we ultimately only live half of the life we really want to.

HOW TO RESOLVE THIS

Healthy emotional processing looks different for everyone but generally involves these steps:

- Get clear on what happened.

- Validate your feelings.

- Determine a course correction.

First, you need to understand why you're upset or the reason why something is bothering you so much. Without clarity on this, you'll continue to waste your time mulling over the details without really understanding what's hurting you so much.

Next, you have to validate how you feel. Recognize that you are not alone; anyone in your situation would probably feel similarly (and does) and that what you feel is absolutely okay. In doing this, you can allow yourself a physical release such as crying, shaking, journaling about what you feel, or talking to a trusted friend.

Once you are clear on what's wrong and have allowed yourself to fully express the extent of your emotions, you can determine how you will change your behavior or thought process so that you get an outcome that you really want in the future.

JUSTIFICATION

Your life is ultimately measured by your outcomes, not your intentions. It is not about what you wanted to do or would have done but didn't have the time. It's not about why you thought you couldn't; it's just whether or not you eventually did. When you're in a pattern of self-sabotaging behavior, you're often treating those excuses the same way you would treat measurable outcomes: You're using them to make yourself feel momentarily satisfied, using them as a replacement for the accomplishment itself.

When we have a goal, dream, or plan, there is no measure of intent. It is only whether you did it or did not. Any other reason you offer for not showing up and doing the work is simply you stating that you prioritize that reason over your ultimate ambition, which means that it will always take precedence in your life.

You may also be using excuses to help navigate away from uncomfortable feelings that are ultimately necessary for your growth.

HOW YOU RESOLVE THIS

Start measuring your outcomes and focusing on at least doing one productive thing each day.

It's no longer about how many days you really wanted to go to the gym; it's about how many days you did. It's no longer about wanting to show up for your friends; it's whether or not you did. It's no longer about the great ideas you had about how to change your business; it's about whether or not you did.

Stop accepting your own excuses. Stop being complacent

with your own justifications. Start quantifying your days by how many healthy, positive things you accomplished, and you will see how quickly you begin to make progress.

DISORGANIZATION

By leaving our lives and spaces in disarray, we are not just mindlessly forgetting to take care of our surroundings. We are often actually creating distractions and chaos that serve an unconscious purpose.

A clean, organized space—both for work and for living—is essential to thriving. This means a tidy home, clothes that are easy to reach and put together each morning, a clean kitchen, and an organized desk. Paperwork should be filed in one space, your bedroom should be calming, and everything should have a "home" that it can return to at the end of the day.

Without cleanliness, we create fewer opportunities for ourselves. Nothing positive, nor beautiful, flows from chaos. Deep down, we know this. Often, when we are self-sabotaging through disorganization, it is because when we are very clean or organized, we get an uneasy feeling. That uneasy feeling is what we are trying to avoid, because it is the recognition that now that everything is in order, we must get to work on doing what we need to do or who we want to become.

When we leave our spaces messy, we are always a few tasks or priorities away from stepping out and showing up.

HOW TO RESOLVE THIS

Like anything, you need to start slow and adjust yourself over time. To declutter and reorganize, start with one room, and if that is too much, try one corner, drawer, or closet. Work on that, and only that, and then implement a routine that maintains the organization.

From there, start arranging your space so that it works for you, not against you. Put something soothing on your bedside table like a diffuser, or create an organized family calendar in the kitchen so appointments and schedules are visible to others. If you have trouble with the mail being disorganized, create a spot for it to go when it comes in each day. If you have trouble with laundry being disorganized, create a system for it and decide on a day or two that you do the wash, and do it in bulk.

You must slowly let yourself get used to working at a clean desk, and eventually it will become second nature. You'll begin to realize that you also feel so much less stressed and much more in control of your life.

It is very hard to show up as the person you want to be when you are surrounded by an environment that makes you feel like a person you aren't.

ATTACHMENT TO WHAT YOU DON'T REALLY WANT

Sometimes, your dreams for your life are adopted from other people's preferences. In other cases, you determine what you want and then you outgrow your old ambitions.

Sometimes, we fight endlessly to try to force ourselves to want something that we do not really want, and it always leaves us empty, because it isn't a genuine desire. This is different than lacking motivation or experiencing resistance. Our inability to perform is not based in fear or lack of skill, it is based in an inherent knowing that this is not what we want for our lives, and perhaps we're feeling lost or unable to change our path.

When you find yourself struggling with something, you have to ask yourself: *Do I actually want to do this?* Do you want the job, or do you just like how the title sounds? Are you in love with the person, or do you like the idea of the relationship? Are you still holding an outdated idea of what your greatest success will be, and if so, what would it look like to let that go?

At the end of the day, self-sabotage sometimes functions to show us that we aren't quite on the right path yet, and that we need to reevaluate to determine what would feel best for our lives, even if that means we disappoint some people or even our younger selves.

We do not have to live the rest of our lives trying to achieve some measure of success we thought was ideal when we were too young to understand who we even were. Our only responsibility is to make decisions for the person we have become.

HOW TO RESOLVE THIS

Be willing to accept that maybe your "success story" doesn't look the way that you once thought it might.

Maybe the kind of success you're really hungry for is to feel at peace each day, or making your life about travel instead of work. Maybe it's about having thriving friendships or a happy relationship. Maybe the business you got into 10 years ago isn't the business you want to be in forever. Maybe the work you thought you'd love isn't coming as naturally to you as you'd hoped.

When we let go of what isn't right for us, we create space to discover what is. However, doing so requires the tremendous courage to put our pride aside and see things for what they really are.

JUDGING OTHERS

We all know that gossiping, or judging other people's lives and choices, is not a healthy or positive way to connect with other people. However, it does far more damage than we realize, as it sets up barriers to our own success.

If we feel bad about not being as successful as another person, we might try to find something negative about them to make ourselves feel better. If we do that every time we come across a person who is more successful than we are, we begin to associate that level of success with being disliked. When it comes time for us to take action to move our lives forward, we're going to resist doing it, because becoming more successful will create a breach in our self-concept.

In other cases, you might have heard people you grew up around villainizing others who had money. They might have said things like, "Ugh, rich people are the worst." Maybe they chalked all wealthy people up to being morally corrupt. This sweeping characterization sealed itself in your subconscious, and now you find yourself sabotaging your own attempts to become financially healthy, because you associate it with guilt and being disliked.

When we set up judgments for others, they become rules that we have to play by, too. By judging others for what we don't have or because we envy them, we sabotage our own lives far more than we ever really hurt anybody else.

HOW TO RESOLVE THIS

Many people say that you have to love yourself first before you can love others, but really, if you learn to love others, you will learn to love yourself.

Practice non-judgment through non-assumption. Instead of reaching a conclusion about a person based on the limited information you have about them, consider that you're not seeing the whole picture and don't know the whole story.

When you are more compassionate about other people's lives, you become more compassionate about your own. When you see someone who has something you want, congratulate them, even if it feels hard at first. It will extend back and open you up to receiving it as well.

PRIDE

Pride is often involved in many of our worst decisions.

Sometimes, we know a relationship is wrong, but the shame of leaving seems worse than staying. Sometimes, we start a business and realize we don't really like it very much or refuse to accept that we need to change or ask for help. In these cases, our pride is getting in the way. We are making decisions based on how we imagine people view our lives, not how they actually are. This is not only inaccurate, but it is also very unhealthy.

HOW TO RESOLVE THIS

To overcome our attachment to pride, we have to start to see ourselves more wholly and honestly.

Instead of thinking that we need to prove to everyone around us how perfect and flawless we are, we can imagine ourselves more realistically: as people who, despite our weaknesses, are trying our best. In the end, it looks far worse to hold onto what's wrong because you care about what others think than it is to let go because that's what's right for you. People will respect you far more if you can acknowledge that you are an imperfect person—like everyone else—learning, adapting, and trying your best.

In reaching this mindset, you also open yourself up to learning. By not assuming you know everything or that you need to seem perfect, you can admit when you're wrong, ask for assistance, and lean on others sometimes. Basically, you open yourself back up to growth, and your life is better for it over the long term.

GUILT OF SUCCEEDING

In a world of so much pain, horror, and misfortune, who are we to have happy, abundant lives?

That's the thought process that so many people go through. One of the biggest mental barriers people face is the guilt that comes with finally having enough or more than one needs. This can come from many different sources, but it ultimately boils down to feeling as though you "don't deserve" to have it.

This feeling often comes up when we start to earn more money or have nicer things. Often, people will sabotage their higher incomes with reckless discretionary spending or by being less vigilant about their clientele or workload, because they are not quite comfortable having more than the basic necessities, and so they put themselves back into a comfortable feeling of lack.

When it comes to success, guilt is an unfortunately common emotion, especially for good-hearted people who want to do the right thing and live authentic lives.

HOW TO RESOLVE THIS

Please realize that most extremely successful people have no guilt whatsoever. In fact, this feeling usually only comes up when you're stepping between not having enough and finally having enough.

What you have to realize is that money and success are tools. They buy you back time and offer you the opportunity to help, employ, influence, and change the lives of others. Instead of looking at your success as a status differentiator—which will always make you feel bad and uncomfortable—see it instead as a tool with which you can do important and positive things in the world and your own life.

FEAR OF FAILING

How often do we not even attempt something because we are afraid to look bad or fail immediately?

The fear of failing is often something that holds people back from putting in the work they would need to become truly great at something, but it can also take another, more insidious form. Once we have established something new in our lives, this fear can come up as a constant irrational worry that we're "missing something," that our partner is being unfaithful, or that we're one misstep away from losing it all.

These catastrophic thoughts happen when we want to shield ourselves from potential loss. They only come up when we finally have something we care enough about and really want to keep.

HOW TO RESOLVE THIS

There is a difference between failing because you are trying something new and daring, and failing because you are *not* showing up, doing the work, or being responsible for your actions.

These are two very different experiences and should be separated in your mind.

As scary as it might be to not be great at something initially, or perhaps even experience a loss, it is even worse to fail by virtue of never trying and always playing small. Failure is inevitable, but you have to make sure it's happening for the right reasons.

When we fail out of negligence, we take a step back. When we fail because we are attempting new feats, we take one step closer to what will work.

DOWNPLAYING

When we downplay our successes in life, we are either trying to make ourselves seem less impressive so others do not feel threatened and therefore like us more, or we are trying to avoid the sense that we have "made it," because we are afraid of peaking.

Though so many of us long for the moment when we feel as though we have finally arrived and achieved the measures of success we so deeply desire, we often receive them only to then feel as though they aren't that great, impressive, or that they don't make us feel as good as we thought they would.

This happens because of downplaying. The idea of having "made it" makes us afraid that we are reaching the pinnacle and therefore will fall off of it. If we acknowledge that we've arrived, what goals remain? It is a feeling akin to death, so we instead find another measure to work toward.

Likewise, when we are around other people, we do not stand firmly in our pride because we are taught it is a bad thing (and when done in an unhealthy way, it is). What we are sensing is the feeling of being "better than" others because we have achieved something. This makes us uncomfortable because we know it's both untrue and unkind.

HOW TO RESOLVE THIS

We can all acknowledge and appreciate other people's diverse accomplishments and talents while still being happy about our own. Instead of shrugging off a compliment, we can respond by saying: "Thank you, I worked very hard, and I'm happy to be here."

If the fear is that we are "peaking" too soon, we have to reform our idea of progress. We do not get better only to get worse again. We do not achieve one thing only to lose it and return to what we were before. That instinct is a self-sabotaging behavior, one that wants to keep us within our old comfort zone.

Instead, we can acknowledge that when one part of our life improves, it radiates out to everything else. When we achieve one thing, we are better equipped for the future. Life tends to gradually get better as we keep working on it; it only gets worse if we accomplish something then shut down because we are intimidated by our own power.

UNHEALTHY HABITS

This is the most common way that people sabotage their own success: by maintaining habits that are actively keeping them away from their goals.

This is when someone declares that they want to be in better shape but doesn't change anything they do each day to facilitate that. Or when they want to make a change professionally but find ways to make it difficult if not impossible for them to actually do it.

At the core of all these behaviors is the fact that one part of our psyche understands that we should be evolving and moving forward with our lives and another part is intimidated by the potential discomfort it would bring. Usually, this culminates in so much inner tension and frustration that a breaking point is reached, and changes are made from there.

However, the goal is to *not* have to get to a crisis point in your life before you can become aware of the ways you're holding yourself back from living peacefully and comfortably.

HOW TO RESOLVE THIS

Define health on your own terms. What does a healthy life look like for you? How would it make you feel, and what would you be doing?

It is difficult to look solely to anyone else's definition of healthfulness, particularly because we are all different people with varying needs, preferences, and schedules.

Instead, figure out what makes you feel best. Decide what combination of healthy eating, exercise, and sleep is right for you, and stick to it. Like so many things, healthy habits are best established gradually. Instead of trying to force yourself to take an hour at the gym at 6 AM, try instead to do 15 minutes, or perhaps swap out with a class you really enjoy, or go at a time that works better for your schedule.

Make it easy for yourself to succeed. Prep your meals or keep water by your desk so you can sip it throughout the day. Gradually recondition yourself to prefer healthy habits, ones that actually work for your lifestyle.

BEING "BUSY"

Another very common way that people sabotage is by distracting themselves to the point of being completely phased out of their lives.

People who are constantly "busy" are running from themselves.

Nobody is "busy" unless they want to be busy, and you will know that because so many people with extremely hectic schedules would never describe themselves that way. This is because being "busy" is not a virtue; it only signals to others that you do not know how to manage your time or your tasks.

Being busy communicates importance; it often makes you seem a little untouchable to others. It also overwhelms the body so that it can only focus on the tasks at hand. Being busy is the ultimate way to distract ourselves from what's really wrong.

HOW TO RESOLVE THIS

If your schedule is unmanageable, you're never going to be as effective or productive as you could be. If this is the case, your first job has to be to streamline and prioritize your tasks in order of importance, outsource whatever else you can, and then let go of the rest.

If your issue is that you intentionally create chaos and busy-ness in your day when there is no need for it, you have to get comfortable with simplicity and routine. Start with writing down your top 5 tasks that need to be done each day, and then focus on doing those and only those.

You might also need to confront the sense of "protection" that being busy gives you. Does it make you feel more important than others? Does it give you an excuse to say "no" to plans or to avoid some people? You need to find healthier and more productive ways to cope with these feelings, such as finding genuine self-confidence in what you do by creating something you're proud of, or getting better at calmly but clearly stating your boundaries and needs in relationships.

SPENDING TIME WITH THE WRONG PEOPLE

It's true that so much of our lives is shaped by the people we spend them with, and the company you keep is another common way that people self-sabotage.

Certainly you can think of some people in your life who stress you out, make you feel insecure, and yet keep you coming back for more. These relationships exist at the lighter end of the toxicity spectrum, but they are self-defeating nonetheless.

If you find yourself preoccupied with a certain friendship or relationship that is making you feel almost addicted to the feeling of being "less than" or "jealous of," you need to gradually phase out of it. You don't need to be mean, rude, or even cut anyone out of your life.

You do, however, need to understand that the people you spend the most time with will shape your future irrevocably, and so you must choose them wisely.

HOW TO RESOLVE THIS

Work on building a circle of people who support and inspire you, who have similar goals and enjoy spending time with you. You should leave a get-together feeling energized and inspired, not exhausted and angry.

It takes time to find your group of friends, and you may not discover that all at once. It could start with offering to take someone you admire out for coffee, or reaching out to do something with a person with whom you'd like to reconnect. Slowly but genuinely rebuild your connections, and then foster and care for them as much as you can.

WORRYING ABOUT IRRATIONAL FEARS AND LEAST LIKELY CIRCUMSTANCES

Another very common way that people sabotage without realizing is by preoccupying themselves with fears of worst-case scenarios.

You're probably familiar with this, at least to some degree: You have a weird or highly unlikely thought that evokes a deep sense of dread, fear, and series of "doomsday" scenarios in your head. You then keep coming back to it to the point that it even controls some part of your life.

Irrational fears, especially the kind that are least likely to become reality, are often what we project real fears onto.

These irrational fears are safe, because deep down we know they aren't going to happen. They are placeholders, a way for us to express the feeling we really have onto something we know isn't going to happen.

When you find yourself in a fear cycle, constantly repeating some strange, random, or unimportant one-off circumstance or situation that has a very low probability of becoming reality, ask yourself if you have any feelings about something related that is actually valid.

For example, if you get anxious about being a passenger in a car, consider if your fear is of "moving forward" or being "out of control." Or, if you're anxious about being fired from your job, the fear might really be the idea that you aren't worthy of another job or being humiliated by a higher-up.

HOW TO RESOLVE THIS

Instead of wasting all of your energy trying to control some wost-case scenario, consider what the message of the fear may be and what it is telling you that you need in your life.

If the fear was an abstract metaphor, what would the meaning be? Is the abrupt loss of income a symbol of your desire for security? Is the fear of the future a symbol for not living fully right now? Is the anxiety about making decisions a symbol for knowing what you really want and being too afraid to choose it?

At the core of the things we most fear is a message that we are trying to send ourselves about what we really care about. If we can identify what we want to protect, we can find healthier and more secure ways to do it.

HOW TO TELL IF YOU'RE IN A SELF-SABOTAGE CYCLE

Even if you can cognitively understand self-sabotaging behaviors, sometimes the most difficult shift is recognizing that we are engaging in them.

In fact, sometimes the signs are so subtle, they are barely recognizable and often don't come to our attention until they become highly problematic or someone else points them out. Some of the most prominent symptoms of self-sabotage are as follows:

YOU ARE MORE AWARE OF WHAT YOU DON'T WANT THAN WHAT YOU DO.

You spend more of your time worrying, ruminating, and focusing on what you hope doesn't happen than you do imagining, strategizing, and planning for what you do.

YOU SPEND MORE TIME TRYING TO IMPRESS PEOPLE WHO DON'T LIKE YOU THAN YOU SPEND WITH PEOPLE WHO LOVE YOU FOR WHO YOU ARE.

You are more focused on growing into the kind of person who evokes the envy of your supposed enemies rather than the kind of person who is beloved by their family and friends and prioritizes them no matter what.

YOU'RE PUTTING YOUR HEAD IN THE SAND.

You don't know basic facts about your life, like how much debt you have or what other people in your field are being paid for similar work. When you get into an argument, you run away until you forget rather than talking about what's wrong and coming up with a solution. In other words, you are in denial, and so any hope of healing is futile.

YOU CARE MORE ABOUT CONVINCING OTHER PEOPLE YOU'RE OKAY THAN ACTUALLY BEING OKAY.

You'd rather post photos that make it look like you had a great time than being concerned about whether you actually had a good time. You put more effort toward trying to convince everyone you're doing well rather than being honest and connecting with people who could help or support you.

YOUR MAIN PRIORITY IN LIFE IS TO BE LIKED, EVEN IF THAT COMES AT THE EXPENSE OF BEING HAPPY.

You think more about whether or not your actions will earn you the approval of "people" (who are "people," by the way?) rather than whether or not they will actually make you feel fulfilled and content with who you are.

YOU'RE MORE AFRAID OF YOUR FEELINGS THAN ANYTHING ELSE.

If you get to the point in life at which the scariest, most detrimental thing you face is the fear of whether or not you will be able to handle your own emotions, you are the one standing in your own way—nothing else is.

YOU'RE BLINDLY CHASING GOALS WITHOUT ASKING YOURSELF WHY YOU WANT THOSE THINGS.

If you are doing "everything you are supposed to be doing" and yet you feel empty and depressed at the end of the day, the issue is probably that you're not really doing what you want to be doing; you've just adopted someone else's script for happiness.

YOU'RE TREATING YOUR COPING MECHANISMS AS THE PROBLEM.

Instead of trying to incite war on yourself to overcome your overeating, spending, drinking, sexing—whatever it is you know you need to improve—ask yourself what emotional need that thing is filling. Until you do, you will battle it forever.

YOU VALUE YOUR DOUBT MORE THAN YOUR POTENTIAL.

Negativity bias makes us believe that "bad" things are more real than good, and unless we keep that inclination in check, it can leave us believing that everything we fear to be true is more real than the good things that are actually true.

YOU ARE TRYING TO CARE ABOUT EVERYTHING.

Your willpower is a limited resource. You only have so much in a day. Rather than using it to try to become good at everything, decide what matters most to you. Focus your attention on that, and let everything else slip away.

YOU ARE WAITING FOR SOMEONE ELSE TO OPEN A DOOR, OFFER APPROVAL, OR HAND YOU THE LIFE YOU HAVE BEEN WAITING FOR.

We grow up with the illusion that success is what's handed to people who are most deserving, talented, or privileged. When we arrive, however, we realize it is constructed by those who find an intersection of their interests, passions, skills, and a market gap. Sprinkle on a little bit of persistence, and the only way to fail is to give up.

YOU DON'T REALIZE HOW FAR YOU'VE COME.

You are not the person you were five years ago. You evolve as your self-image does, so make sure that it's an accurate one. Give yourself credit for everything you've overcome that you never thought you would, and everything you've built that you never thought you could. You've come so much farther than you think, and you're so much closer than you realize.

IDENTIFYING YOUR SUBCONSCIOUS COMMITMENTS

Part of the reason we often experience intense inner conflict or self-sabotage is because of something called a core commitments, which is essentially your primary objective or intention for your life.[5]

Your subconscious commitments are basically what you want more than anything else, and you often aren't even aware of them. You can identify your core commitments by looking at the things that you struggle with most and the things you are most driven by. If you can peel back the layers of your motivations toward each, you'll find a root cause. When you find the same root cause for everything, you've found a core commitment.

People only seem irrational and unpredictable until you understand what they are fundamentally committed to.

For example, if someone has a core commitment to feel free, they may find themselves sabotaging work opportunities in order to achieve that. If someone's core commitment is to feel wanted, they could find themselves in a series of relationships in which they have intense connections but refuse to make commitments out of fear that the spark will "fade." If someone's core commitment is to be in control of their lives, they might have irrational anxiety about things that *represent* a loss of control. If someone's core commitment is to be loved by others, they might pretend to be helpless in certain areas of life because if they don't *need* others, they might be *left* by them.

But the most important thing to understand is that your core commitments are actually a cover-up for core needs. Your core need is the opposite of your core commitment. Your core need is also another way to identify your *purpose.* For example, if your subconscious core commitment is to be in control, your core need is trust. If your subconscious core commitment is to be needed, your core need is to know you are wanted. If your subconscious core commitment is to be loved by others, your need is self-love.

> The less that you feed your core need, the "louder" your core commitment symptoms will be.

If you are a person who needs trust and is therefore committed to staying in control, the less that you believe you are supported, the more your negative coping mechanisms are going to flare up. Perhaps this could happen in the form of disruptive eating patterns, isolating yourself, or hyper-fixation on physical appearance. If you are committed to freedom and therefore need a sense of autonomy, the less that you build a life on your own terms, the more you are going to sabotage opportunities and feel drained and exhausted when you "should" feel happy.

The more you lean into fulfilling your core needs, the more your commitment symptoms will disappear.

Once you understand what a person really wants, you will be able to explain the intricacies of their habits and behaviors. You will be able to predict down to the detail what they will do in any given situation. More importantly, once you start asking yourself what you really want, you'll be able to stop battling the symptoms and start addressing the only issue that has ever really existed in your life, which is living out of alignment with your core needs and, therefore, your core purpose.

CONFRONTING REPRESSED EMOTIONS AND TAKING ACTION

There is a difference between understanding why we self-sabotage and the act of no longer self-sabotaging.

This means that once we understand the root and purpose of the behavior, we adjust it. We adapt. Overcoming self-sabotage is not just a matter of understanding why you're holding yourself back; it is being able to take action in the direction that you want and need to, even if it is initially uncomfortable or triggering.

This is a very important part of the process, because you are essentially going to be confronting the exact emotions you have been trying to avoid.

When you stop engaging in self-sabotaging behavior, repressed emotions that you weren't even aware of will start to come up, and you might feel even worse than you did before.

The thing about overcoming self-sabotage is that we don't often need to be told what to do. We know what we want to do, and we know what we need to do. It is simply that we are being held back by our fear of feeling. To begin to unravel this emotional holding pattern, we can work through the following to find more ease and space and freedom while we change our lives.

THE MOST COMMON EMOTIONS THAT ARISE WHILE YOU'RE BREAKING SELF-SABOTAGING BEHAVIORS

The first feeling you are likely to confront is resistance. This is that generalized sense of being "stuck" or your body feeling so tense that it is almost "hard," as though you are hitting a wall. This feeling is usually a masking emotion that is preventing you from actually being aware of the sensations beneath it which are more acute.

When you start to feel resistance, you don't want to just "push through it." In fact, trying to do that means you'll keep hitting the same wall that you're up against already. You're going to strengthen the self-sabotaging behavior because you aren't really solving the problem by just trying to override it.

Instead, start asking the right questions.

Why do I feel this way?

What is this feeling trying to tell me about the action I am trying to take?

Is there something I need to learn here?

What do I need to do to honor my needs right now?

Then you have to reconnect to your inspiration or your vision for life. Get clear on *why* you want to take this action and make a change. When your motivation is the fact that you want to live a different and better existence, you're going to find that a lot of the resistance fades because you're being pushed by a vision that's greater than your fear.

In other cases, you might run into other emotions such as anger, sadness, or inadequacy. When those feelings come up, it is very important to make space for them. This means to allow them to rise up in your body and observe them. Watch where they make you tense up or constrict. Feel what they want you to feel. There is nothing worse than the fear of feeling the emotion, as the experience itself is ultimately often just some physical tension around which we've crafted a story.

Remember that a lot of these feelings may very well have a root in something related to the self-sabotaging behavior. If you are angry about how one of your parents treated you, it probably won't come as a surprise that the core feeling of why you are sabotaging your relationships is anger and mistrust. The feelings associated with self-sabotage are not usually random. In fact, they can lead us to deeper insights about what we really need and what problems within us are still unresolved.

To fully release those feelings once you are aware of them, try writing yourself a letter. Write something to your younger self or from the perspective of your future self. Write down a mantra or a manifesto. Remind yourself that you love yourself too much to settle for less, or that it is okay to be angry in unfair or frustrating circumstances. Give yourself space to experience the depth of your emotions so that they do not control your behaviors.

DISCONNECTING ACTION AND FEELING

The final and most important lesson to overcome self-sabotage is to learn to disconnect action from feeling.

We are not held back in life because we are incapable of making change. We are held back because we don't *feel like* making change, and so we don't.

The truth is that you can have a vision of what you want, know that it is undoubtedly right for you, and simply not feel like taking the action required to pursue that path.

This is because our feelings are essentially wired as comfort systems. They produce a "good" feeling when we are doing what we have always done—staying in familiarity. This, to our bodies, registers as "safety." In other cases, the accomplishments or changes that we are very happy about are those that we also perceive to offer us a greater measure of safety. If the achievement potentially puts us at risk in any way or exposes us to something unfamiliar, we aren't going to be happy about it initially, even if it is a net positive for our lives.

However, we can actually train ourselves to prefer behaviors that are good for us. This is how we restructure our comfort zones. We begin to crave what we repeatedly do, but the first few times we do it, we often feel uncomfortable. The trick is being able to override that initial hesitation so we are guiding our lives with logic and reason, not emotionality.

Though your emotions are always valid and need to be validat*ed*, they are hardly ever an accurate measure of what you are capable of in life. They are not always an accurate reflection of reality. All your feelings know is what you've done in the past, and they are attached to what they've drawn comfort from.

You may feel as though you are worthless, but you most certainly are not. You may feel as though there is no hope, but there most certainly is. You may feel as though everyone dislikes you, but that is probably a gross overexaggeration. You may think everyone is judging you, but that is a misperception.

Most importantly, you may feel as though you *cannot* take action, when you most certainly can. You simply do not feel *willing,* because you are not used to it.

By using logic and vision to guide ourselves, we are able to identify a different and better life experience. When we imagine this, we feel peaceful and inspired. To rise up to meet this version of our lives, we must overcome our resistance and discomfort. We will not feel happy *initially,* no matter how "right" for us those actions are.

It is essential that you learn to take action before you feel like doing it. Taking action builds momentum and creates motivation. These feelings will not come to you spontaneously; you have to generate them. You have to inspire yourself, you have to move. You have to simply begin and allow your life and your energy to reorient itself to prefer the behaviors that are going to move your life forward, not the ones that are keeping you held back.

CHAPTER 3

YOUR TRIGGERS ARE THE GUIDES TO YOUR FREEDOM

NOW THAT YOU HAVE BEGUN to identify your self-sabotaging behaviors, you can use them to uncover deeper and more important truths about who you are as a person and what you really want and need out of life.

This is an important part of the process, because overcoming our self-defeating habits is not just about knowing what they are or why we engage in them. It is also about better understanding what our inherent needs are, what we really desire, and how we can use this as a pivot point to begin building a life that is aligned with who we really are and what we are here to do.

Our triggers do not actually exist just to show us where we are storing unresolved pain. In fact, they show us something much deeper.

Each "negative" emotion we experience comes with a message, one that we do not yet know how to interpret. This is when a single challenge begins to become a chronic issue. Unable to honor and use the guidance of the emotion, we shut the feeling down, store it in our bodies, and try to avoid anything that might bring it up again. This is when we become sensitive to the world around us, because there are a lot of repressed feelings mounting.

On the surface, it seems as though the thing that triggers our emotional response is the problem. It is not. The problem is that we don't know what to do with how we feel and therefore do not have all of the emotional processing skills that we need.

When we can identify *why* something is triggering us, we can use the experience as a catalyst for a release and positive life change.

HOW TO INTERPRET NEGATIVE EMOTIONS

Though everyone's particular triggers are unique to them, it helps to better understand the function of some of the feelings that we often condemn.

Some of the emotions that are most strongly connected with self-sabotaging behaviors are actually important for us to better understand. It is not about simply "getting over" them; it is about listening to what they are trying to tell us about our experience.

ANGER

Anger is a beautiful, transformative emotion. It is mischaracterized by its shadow side, aggression, and therefore we try to resist it.

It is healthy to be angry, and anger can also show us important aspects of who we are and what we care about. For example, anger shows us where our boundaries are. Anger also helps us identify what we find to be unjust.

Ultimately, anger is trying to mobilize us, to initiate action. Anger is transformative, and it is often the peak state we reach before we truly change our lives. This is because anger is not intended to be projected onto someone else; rather, it's an influx of motivation that helps us change what we need to change within our lives. When we do not see it as such, we tend to bury it, not ever resolving the real issue at hand. This is when anger starts to cross over into aggression—when we take that energy out on those around us as opposed to using it as an impetus to change ourselves.

Instead of being afraid of anger, we can instead use it to help us see our limits and priorities more clearly. We can also use it to help us make big, important changes both for ourselves and the world around us.

SADNESS

Sadness is the normal and correct response to the loss of something you very much love.

This is an emotion that often comes up in the aftermath of a disappointment. This could be the loss of a relationship, a job, or just a general idea of what you thought your life would be.

Sadness only becomes problematic when we do not allow ourselves to go through the natural phases of grief. Sadness does not release itself all at once. In fact, we often find that it happens in waves, some of which strike us at unexpected times.

We do not ever need to feel embarrassed or wrong for needing to cry, feel down, or miss what we no longer have. In fact, crying at appropriate times is one of the biggest signs of mental strength, as people who are struggling often find it difficult to release their feelings and be vulnerable.

GUILT

Guilt tends to affect us more for what we *didn't* do than what we did. In fact, people who struggle the most with guilt are the people who are not actually guilty of something terrible. People who commit heinous acts tend to not feel much remorse. The fact that you feel bad that you could have done wrong by someone is a good sign in itself.

However, guilt requires us to look deeply at what behaviors, if any, we feel badly about, as well as what we may have done that was not in our best interest. If we have treated others unfairly, we must be able to admit, apologize, and correct that behavior. However, if the feeling of guilt is more generalized and not specifically relating to any one incident, we need to look closely at who or what made us always feel as though we were "wrong" or inconveniencing others.

Guilt is often an emotion we carry from childhood and then project onto current circumstances when we felt as though we were burdens to those around us.

EMBARRASSMENT

Embarrassment is what we feel when we know that we did not behave in a way that we are proud of.

Other people can never make us feel as embarrassed as we make ourselves feel. When you are truly and completely confident that you are doing the best you can with what you have in front of you, you stop feeling embarrassed all the time. Sure, others can make you feel bad with their comments or ideas, but even their worst judgments tend to be neutralized when we accept ourselves and feel proud of who we are.

Shame is the shadow side of embarrassment. This is when the natural, occasional feeling of being embarrassed turns into a way for us to completely condemn ourselves as human beings and begin to see ourselves as worthless and invalid.

When we do not process the feeling of embarrassment, it tends to turn into something far darker.

JEALOUSY

Jealousy is a cover-up emotion. It presents as anger or judgment, when in reality it is sadness and self-dissatisfaction.

If you want to know what you truly want out of life, look at the people who you are jealous of. No, you may not want *exactly* what they have, but the feeling that you are experiencing is anger that they are allowing themselves to pursue it while you are not.

When we use our jealousy to judge other people's accomplishments, we are siding into its shadow function. When we use our jealousy to show us what we would like to accomplish, we begin to recognize the self-sabotaging behavior and get ready to commit to what we actually desire.

You can think of it this way: When we see someone who has something we really want but we are suppressing our willingness to pursue it, we must also condemn it in them so we can justify our own course of action. Instead of this, we can see what we'd also like to create.

RESENTMENT

When we resent people, it is often because they did not live up to the expectation of them that we had in our minds.

Resentment in some ways is like a projected regret. Instead of trying to show us what *we* should change, it seems to want to tell us what *other people* should change. However, other people are under no obligation to live up to our ideas of them. In fact, our only problem is that we have an unrealistic expectation that someone was meant to be exactly as we think they should or love us exactly as we imagined they would.

When we are faced with resentment, what we instead must do is reinvent our image of those around us or those we have perceived as having wronged us. Other people are not here to love us perfectly; they are here to teach us lessons to show us how to love them—and ourselves—better.

When we release the ideas we have about who they should be, we can see them for who they are and the role they are meant to play in our lives. Instead of focusing on how they should change, we can focus instead on what we can learn.

REGRET

Much like jealousy, regret is also another way that we show ourselves not what we wish we could have done in the past, but what we absolutely need to create going forward.

The truth is that most people regret what they did *not* do more than they ever regret what they did. This isn't a coincidence. Regret isn't actually trying to just make us feel bad that we didn't live up to our own expectations. It is trying to motivate us to live up to them going forward. It is trying to show us what it is absolutely imperative to change in the future and what we really care about experiencing before we die.

Didn't travel when you were young? Regret is showing you that you should do it now. Didn't look as nice as you wanted to? Regret is showing you that you should try harder. Made choices that didn't reflect your best self? Regret is showing you that you should make different ones now. Didn't love someone while you had them? Regret is showing you that you should appreciate people now.

CHRONIC FEAR

When we cannot stop returning to fearful thoughts, it is not always because there is an actual threat in front of us. Often, it is because our internal response systems are underdeveloped or sidelined by trauma.

When we are in a state of fearful thinking, it doesn't matter what we are afraid of; the thought process follows us from problem to problem. Often, there's a metaphor encoded within it. For example, we may be afraid of an ultimate "loss of control" or some external force coming in and unraveling our progress.

Regardless, chronic fearful thinking often comes back down to feeling the need to focus our energy and attention on a potential threat so we can protect ourselves from it. We imagine that if we are worried, anxious, or angry about it, it will remain within our awareness and therefore cannot surprise us. We can retain some control over it.

The very act of holding these fearful thoughts within our minds is exactly how the fear is controlling us in the first place. It is derailing our lives *right now,* because we are channeling our energy into something that is outside of our control, as opposed to using it for everything that is actually within our control—the habits, actions, and behaviors that would actually move our lives forward.

In this sense, what we are afraid of is really a projection of what's already happening.

The only true way to get over chronic fear is actually to get *through* it. Instead of trying to battle, resist, and avoid what we cannot control, we can learn to simply shrug and say, and *if that happens, it happens.* The second we are able to shrug, laugh, or even just throw our hands up and say,

"Whatever, it will be fine," we instantly take back all of our power.

What keeps the fire of fear raging is the idea that if we accept what we are afraid of, we are giving in to the worst potential outcome. The truth is that when we stop being afraid of what we cannot control and know instead that *nothing* can possibly ruin our lives more than *we* are ruining them with our negative, distracted, and irrational thinking and focus, we are completely freed.

When we are in full acceptance, fear leaves our consciousness and becomes a non-issue. It is at this point we realize that it always was.

OUR INTERNAL GUIDANCE SYSTEMS WHISPER UNTIL THEY SCREAM

The things that are bothering you most right now are not external forces trying to torture you for the sake of it—they are your own mind identifying what in your life can be fixed, changed, and transformed. If you continue to not take action, the siren will only get louder, and if you never learn to listen to it, you will probably just disassociate from it and then be a victim to it.

You already have the answers. You already know what you're here to do. You are here to create everything that would make you happier than you can imagine. It is only a matter of quieting your mind enough so you can feel all of the unlimited potential that is begging you to be used.

There's no such thing as self-sabotage because the behaviors that you think are holding you back are really just meeting your needs. It's not a matter of trying to push yourself beyond them; it's a matter of seeing them for what they are and then finding better, healthier ways to fulfill them.

Though we live in an age where people tend to tell us that we should be entirely self-sufficient, and to want or need another person's presence, validation, or company is a sign of self-insufficiency, that is not an accurate portrayal of what it means to be human, and it severely overlooks the reality of human nature and connection.

Though many people are codependent and lean far too heavily on others to give them a sense of safety and self, leaning too far the other way—where you believe that you don't need anyone or anything and that you can do everything yourself—is not healthy, either. They are two opposite manifestations of the same wounds, which are mistrust and the inability to connect.

Your need to feel validated is valid.

Your need to feel the presence of another person is valid.

Your need to feel wanted is valid.

Your need to feel secure is valid.

Often, the first reason we start neglecting our essential needs is because we think we are weak for having them. We only believe this because when we were young we did have to rely almost entirely on others to meet our essential needs. Eventually, this fails us, because another person cannot fulfill us entirely, nor are they responsible for it. As we grow up, we learn self-sufficiency. In fact, reliance on oneself for the foundation of our basic needs is an important part of a person's development.

In the same way, it is also important that we recognize we cannot meet *every single one* of our needs on our own.

Human beings are hardwired for connection to others and to a group. This is why we exist in subsets, like communities, and families, and generally feel happiest and most fulfilled when we are doing things that serve the greater good. This is a fundamental and healthy part of who we are, and it is not a sign of weakness.

In other cases, your need to feel financially secure is healthy; it is not always a product of you being greedy or ill-intentioned. Your need to be validated for the work that you do is healthy, and it is not always a product of you being vain. Your need to live in a space and area that you enjoy being in is healthy, and it is not always a product of you being ungrateful for what you have.

YOUR SUBCONSCIOUS MIND IS TRYING TO COMMUNICATE WITH YOU

Within our self-sabotaging behaviors lies incredible wisdom. Not only can they tell us how and what we have been traumatized by, they can also show us what we really need. Embedded within each self-sabotaging behavior is actually the key to unlock it, if only we can understand it first.

These are a few brief examples of how your subconscious mind might be trying to communicate with you through your behaviors.

THE WAY YOU ARE SELF-SABOTAGING: Going back to the same person who broke you in a relationship. This could be a platonic friend but is most commonly a former romantic partner.

WHAT YOUR SUBCONSCIOUS MIND MIGHT WANT YOU TO KNOW: It could be time to evaluate your childhood relationships. If you find something comforting or appealing about someone who hurts you, there's usually a reason.

THE WAY YOU ARE SELF-SABOTAGING: Attracting people who are too broken to commit in a real way.

WHAT YOUR SUBCONSCIOUS MIND MIGHT WANT YOU TO KNOW: You are not too broken to find someone who actually wants you, and when you begin to recognize that you are worthy of being committed to, you'll start choosing partners who do just that.

THE WAY YOU ARE SELF-SABOTAGING: Feeling unhappy, even if nothing is wrong, and really, you've gotten everything you've wanted in life.

WHAT YOUR SUBCONSCIOUS MIND MIGHT WANT YOU TO KNOW: You are probably expecting outside things to make you feel good rather than relying on changing how you think and what you focus on. No outward accomplishment is going to give you a true and lasting sense of inner peace, and your discomfort, despite your accomplishments, is calling your attention to that.

THE WAY YOU ARE SELF-SABOTAGING: Pushing people away.

WHAT YOUR SUBCONSCIOUS MIND MIGHT WANT YOU TO KNOW: You want people to love and accept you so much that the stress of it all makes you isolate yourself from the pain, effectively creating the reality you're trying to avoid. Alternatively, needing solitude too often usually means there is a discrepancy between who you pretend to be and who you actually are. When you show up to your life more authentically, it becomes easier to have people around you, as it requires less effort.

THE WAY YOU ARE SELF-SABOTAGING: Automatically believing what you think and feel is true.

WHAT YOUR SUBCONSCIOUS MIND MIGHT WANT YOU TO KNOW: You want to worry because it feels comfortable, and therefore safer. The more you blindly trust every random thought or feeling that passes through you, the more you are going to be at the whim of what's happening around you. You must learn to steady yourself in clarity, truth, and groundedness, and to be able to mentally discern between what is helpful and what is not.

THE WAY YOU ARE SELF-SABOTAGING: Eating poorly when you don't want to.

WHAT YOUR SUBCONSCIOUS MIND MIGHT WANT YOU TO KNOW: You are doing too much, or you're not giving yourself enough rest and nourishment. You are being too extreme. This is why your body is requiring that you continue to fuel it. Alternatively, it could be that you are emotionally hungry, and because you are not giving yourself the true experiences you crave, you are satisfying your "hunger" another way.

THE WAY YOU ARE SELF-SABOTAGING: Not doing the work you know would help move your career forward.

WHAT YOUR SUBCONSCIOUS MIND MIGHT WANT YOU TO KNOW: You might not be as clear as you think you are on what you want to be doing. If it isn't flowing, there is a reason. Instead of trying to push through and continually hitting the same wall over and over again, take a step back. Maybe it's time to regroup, restrategize, or seriously think about why you're trying to take the steps you are. Something needs to change, and it's probably not just your motivation.

THE WAY YOU ARE SELF-SABOTAGING: Overworking.

WHAT YOUR SUBCONSCIOUS MIND MIGHT WANT YOU TO KNOW: You do not have to prove your value. You do, however, have to stop running from the discomfort of being alone with your feelings, which is very often the reason that people overwork. There is a difference between being passionately committed to something and feeling obligated to outperform everyone else. One is healthy; the other is not.

THE WAY YOU ARE SELF-SABOTAGING: Caring too much about what other people think.

WHAT YOUR SUBCONSCIOUS MIND MIGHT WANT YOU TO KNOW: You are not as happy as you think you are. The happier you are with something, the less you need other people to be. Instead of wondering whether or not someone else will think you are enough, stop and ask yourself: *Is my life enough for me?* How do you really feel about your life when you aren't looking at it through the eyes of others?

THE WAY YOU ARE SELF-SABOTAGING: Spending too much money.

WHAT YOUR SUBCONSCIOUS MIND MIGHT WANT YOU TO

KNOW: Things will not make you feel more secure. You will not be able to purchase your way into a new life or identity. If you are overspending or spending outside of your means on a regular basis to the point that it is detrimental to you, you need to look at what function buying or shopping serves. Is it a distraction, a replacement for a hobby, or an addiction to the feeling of being "renewed" in some way? Determine what your needs really are, and then go from there.

THE WAY YOU ARE SELF-SABOTAGING: Dwelling on past relationships or continually checking up on exes.

WHAT YOUR SUBCONSCIOUS MIND MIGHT WANT YOU TO KNOW: This relationship affected you more than you are letting yourself believe. The ending hurt you more than you acknowledged, and you need to process that. Your continued interest in this person means there's something about the relationship that is still unresolved, and it is probably some kind of closure or acceptance that you need to find for yourself.

THE WAY YOU ARE SELF-SABOTAGING: Choosing friends who always make you feel like you're in competition with them.

WHAT YOUR SUBCONSCIOUS MIND MIGHT WANT YOU TO KNOW: Wanting to feel "better" than people is not a replacement for needing to feel connected to them, but that's often how we use it. We do this not because we actually want to be superior, but because we want to seem valuable and valued. What we want is authentic connection and to feel important to others, but making them feel inferior is not the way to accomplish it.

THE WAY YOU ARE SELF-SABOTAGING: Having self-defeating thoughts that hold you back from doing what you want.

WHAT YOUR SUBCONSCIOUS MIND MIGHT WANT YOU TO KNOW: Being mean to yourself first will not make it hurt less if other people judge or reject you, though that is why you are using this defense mechanism. Thinking the worst of yourself is a way of trying to numb yourself to what you really fear, which is that someone else could say those things about you. What you don't realize is that you're acting as your own bully and enemy by doing it to yourself. What could someone else's judgment realistically do to your life? Honestly, it could stop you from pursuing your dreams, ambitions, and personal happiness. And that's exactly what you're doing when you stay fixated on those damaging ideas. It's time to get out of your own way.

THE WAY YOU ARE SELF-SABOTAGING: Not promoting your work in a way that would help move you forward.

WHAT YOUR SUBCONSCIOUS MIND MIGHT WANT YOU TO KNOW: You're not creating the best possible work you can, and you sense it. The reason why you're holding back is a fear of judgment, but that wouldn't exist if you weren't already judging yourself. You have to create things you are proud to share, and when sharing them in a positive way that helps grow your business or career feels natural and authentic, you will know that you are doing the work that is at the best of your ability or potential.

THE WAY YOU ARE SELF-SABOTAGING: Ascribing intent or worrying that things are about you when they aren't.

WHAT YOUR SUBCONSCIOUS MIND MIGHT WANT YOU TO KNOW: You think about yourself too often. Other people's lives do not revolve around you, nor do their thoughts. They are busy thinking about themselves in the same way that you are thinking about yourself. Remember that patterns in your life are indicative of your own behaviors, but imagining that every time someone cuts you off in traffic is a personal attack, you're going to severely hold yourself back, because you'll always be the victim of something.

THE WAY YOU ARE SELF-SABOTAGING: Staying in a city or town you claim to dislike.

WHAT YOUR SUBCONSCIOUS MIND MIGHT WANT YOU TO KNOW: Home is where you make it, not where you find it. Is this an issue of you being unable to move, or are you simply unwilling? Usually when we stay in the same place, there's a reason. There's something we love about it, and it's where want to spend our lives. The resistance comes in because of the judgment we imagine others may think if they know we don't live in the coolest, biggest, or the best area. You might also fear that people will judge you for not having "progressed" enough. The truth is that *you* are judging yourself, and you need to make peace or take pride in why you choose to live where you do.

THE WAY YOU ARE SELF-SABOTAGING: Mindlessly scrolling through social media as a way to pass the time.

WHAT YOUR SUBCONSCIOUS MIND MIGHT WANT YOU TO KNOW: This is one of the easiest ways to numb yourself, because it is so accessible and addictive. There is a world-altering difference between using social media in a healthy way versus as a coping mechanism. Mostly, it has to do with how you feel after you're finished. If you don't put the phone down feeling inspired or relaxed, you're probably trying to avoid some kind of discomfort within yourself—the very discomfort that just might be telling you that you need to change.

LEARNING TO LISTEN AGAIN

Now that you're starting to pay attention to your internal cues, it is important to understand how to listen to yourself and respond in real time.

You are in the situation you are in now because you did not know how to understand or meet your needs in the moment. If you do not want to constantly have to be "fixing" your choices and behaviors, you have to learn how to process and interpret your feelings in real time. This will be done by a process of building emotional intelligence, which will be primarily done in the next chapter. However, this is where we begin: by understanding how to listen to our instincts.

HOW TO FOLLOW YOUR "GUT" WITHOUT GETTING SCARED OF THE FUTURE

One of the most essential tenets of modern wisdom is the idea that deep down, you know the truth about everything in your life and, by extension, your future. The idea is that you are an oracle unto yourself, and your feelings are apertures into not only what's happening now, but what's going to happen soon.

We're not to blame for believing this. There's a significant amount of research that proves the interconnectedness of our brains and bodies—explaining why when we have a "gut feeling" or an instinct that precedes logic, it is often correct.

This is because the lining of our gastrointestinal system functions as a "second brain," given how it stores a backlog of information that your conscious mind can't recall faster than your body can sense. It is this incredible skill that makes your instinct almost always correct.

Your gut—though intelligent—isn't psychic.

If you want to tune into yourself more, follow your heart, pursue your passion, find your soul—whatever it is—the first thing that you have to understand is that your "gut instinct" can only respond to what's happening in the present. If you have an "instinct" about a future event, you're projecting.

This is how you can start breaking down your "gut feelings." Are you responding to someone who is in front of you, or are you responding to your idea of them in your head? Are you reacting to a situation that's playing out right now, or are you reacting to one you imagine, assuming you know how it will go? Are your feelings regarding what's happening right now or what you hope and fear will happen in the future?

Aside from only really being able to function in the present, your gut instinct is also quiet. The "little voice" within is just that… little.

It does not scream. It does not panic. It does not pump your body with adrenaline to get your attention. It is not angry. It is the wave of clarity that overcomes you in the middle of your darkest moments, in which something tells you: *It's going to be all right; it's not as bad as you think, everything is okay.*

Your gut instinct functions to make things better, whereas your imagination can often make things worse.

But this is often confusing to people, because which feelings are your instincts, and what are your fears, or doubts, or limiting beliefs? How do we know the difference?

Well, your instincts aren't actually feelings; they are responses.

If you find yourself particularly drained after spending time with someone or are feeling like you don't want to see them again, that's your instinct. If the work that you do exhausts you and every bit of it is forced and undesirable, that is your instinct. Instinct is not a feeling (you don't have an "instinct" that you're sad today); instinct is quickly moving yourself out of harm's way without having to think about it.

You have to remember that your feelings, while valid, are not often real. They are not always accurate reflections of reality. They are, however, always accurate reflections of our thoughts. Our thoughts change our feelings. Our thoughts do not change our instincts. What you naturally gravitate toward or away from is your instinct. It's not something you feel or interpret; it's something you naturally do.

When people talk about using their instincts to craft a life they love, this is what they mean: that they are obeying what their subtle intuition tells them they feel best doing. Sometimes, your instinct can move you toward your art, even if it makes you uncomfortable and resistant.

Sometimes, your instinct can move you to keep working on a relationship, even when it's hard.

Your instinct doesn't exist to ensure you feel comfortable and ecstatic at all hours of the day. It moves you toward what you're meant to do, because it shows you where your interests, skills, and desires intersect.

INSTINCT AND FEAR CAN FEEL SIMILAR

To trust your gut is not to treat it as an oracle.

This is when the concept becomes so problematic. We are not only believing random feelings *blindly,* but also applying future meaning to them, assuming that everything we feel is actually warning us or showing us what's ahead.

Let's unpack why and how this happens and how you can prevent it from ruining your life.

Feelings do not inform you of the right decision to make.

Right decisions create the right feelings.

Your feelings are not intended to guide you throughout life; that is what your mind is for.

If you were to honestly follow your every impulse, you would be completely stuck, complacent, and possibly dead or at the very least in severe trouble. You aren't, because your brain is able to intervene and instruct you on how to make choices that reflect what you want to be experiencing long-term.

You begin experiencing feelings of peace and joy in your life when you condition yourself to take repeated daily actions that facilitate clarity, calmness, healthfulness, and purposefulness, not the other way around.

If you want to master your life, you have to learn to organize your feelings. By becoming aware of them, you can trace them back to the thought process that prompted them, and from there you can decide whether or not the idea is an actual threat or concern, or a fabrication of your reptilian mind just trying to keep you alive.

Remember: Your brain was built for nature. Your body was designed to survive in the wild. You have an animalistic form trying to navigate a highly civilized, modern world. Forgive yourself for having these impulses, and at the same time, understand that your choices are ultimately yours. You can feel something and not act on it.

SO WHY ARE WE EVEN TOLD TO "LISTEN TO OUR INSTINCTS" IN THE FIRST PLACE?

Your gut is deeply connected to your mind. There's a physiological connection between your gastrointestinal system and serotonin production in your brain. Your vagus nerve runs from your gut to your head, acting as a communication device to help your system regulate.[6]

Your stomach and your mind are inherently connected, which is why people allude to just knowing something "deep down" or explain that when they're upset, they're "sick to their stomach" or had a "gut reaction" to something.

What isn't being addressed is the fact that listening to your instinct is something that happens in the present moment. You cannot have an instinct about a future event, because it doesn't exist yet. You can have a fear-based or memory response that you are projecting into the future, but you cannot instinctively know something about another person or a future event until it is in front of you.

When you have a "gut instinct" about someone, it is after interacting with them. When you know whether or not a job is right for you, it is only after having done it for a while.

The problem is that we are trying to use our instincts as fortune-telling mechanisms, our brain's creative way of trying to manipulate our body to help us avoid pain and increase pleasure in the future. But that's not what happens. We end up stuck because we are literally trusting every single thing that we feel instead of discerning what's an actual reaction and what's a projection.

IDENTIFYING THE DIFFERENCE BETWEEN INSTINCT AND FEAR

First and foremost, understand that your instinct can serve you immensely in the present moment. Your first reaction to something is very often the wisest reaction, because your body is using all of the subconscious information you have logged away to inform you about something before your brain has an opportunity to second-guess it.

You can use this to your advantage by staying in the moment and asking yourself what is true right here and right now. What is true when you are with another person, activity, or behavior? What is the deep, gut instinct that you get when you're presently engaging with something?

Does it differ from what you think and feel about it when you are just imagining it, making guesses about it, recalling details of it, or imagining what it will be like? Typically, those projections are fear, and your present reaction is your honest instinct.

Overall, your honest gut instinct won't ever frighten you into panic. Your gut is always subtle and gentle, even if it's telling you that something isn't for you. If your gut wants you to know not to see someone or to stop engaging in a relationship or behavior, the impulse will be quiet. That's why it's called the "little voice" within. So easy to miss. So easy to shout over.

INTUITIVE NUDGES VS. INTRUSIVE THOUGHTS

When you start listening to yourself, you might find it hard to tell the difference between thoughts that are helpful and intuitive, and thoughts that are damaging and intrusive. They both function similarly—they are immediate, reactive, and offer some kind of previously unseen insight—and yet they function so completely differently in practice.

This is how to start telling the difference between thoughts that are informed by your intuition and thoughts that are informed by fear:

- Intuitive thoughts are calm. Intruding thoughts are hectic and fear-inducing.

- Intuitive thoughts are rational; they make a degree of sense. Intruding thoughts are irrational and often stem from aggrandizing a situation or jumping to the worst conclusion possible.

- Intuitive thoughts help you in the present. They give you information that you need to make a better-informed decision. Intruding thoughts are often random and have nothing to do with what's going on in the moment.

- Intuitive thoughts are "quiet"; intruding thoughts are "loud," which makes one harder to hear than the other.

- Intuitive thoughts usually come to you once, maybe twice, and they induce a feeling of understanding. Intruding thoughts tend to be persistent and induce a feeling of panic.

- Intuitive thoughts often sound loving, while invasive thoughts sound scared.

- Intuitive thoughts usually come out of nowhere; invasive thoughts are usually triggered by external stimuli.

- Intuitive thoughts don't need to be grappled with—you have them and then you let them go. Invasive thoughts begin a whole spiral of ideas and fears, making it feel impossible to stop thinking about them.

- Even when an intuitive thought doesn't tell you something you like, it never makes you feel panicked. Even if you experience sadness or disappointment, you don't feel overwhelmingly anxious. Panic is the emotion you experience when you don't know what to do with a feeling. It is what happens when you have an invasive thought.

- Intuitive thoughts open your mind to other possibilities; invasive thoughts close your heart and make you feel stuck or condemned.

- Intuitive thoughts come from the perspective of your

best self; invasive thoughts come from the perspective of your most fearful, small self.

- Intuitive thoughts solve problems; invasive thoughts create them.

- Intuitive thoughts help you help others; invasive thoughts tend to create a "me vs. them" mentality.

- Intuitive thoughts help you understand what you're thinking and feeling; invasive thoughts assume what other people are thinking and feeling.

- Intuitive thoughts are rational; invasive thoughts are irrational.

- Intuitive thoughts come from a deeper place within you and give you a resounding feeling deep in your gut; invasive thoughts keep you stuck in your head and give you a panicked feeling.

- Intuitive thoughts show you how to respond; invasive thoughts demand that you react.

HOW TO START TRULY MEETING YOUR NEEDS

Though the term self-care has become an umbrella term that more often refers to behaviors that distract one from the actual problem at hand rather than really taking action to fix the problem at hand, actual self-care is the most fundamental aspect of meeting your own needs.

Aside from your own basic security, your needs are to be nourished, to sleep well, to live in a clean environment, to dress appropriately, and to allow yourself to feel what you feel without judgment or suppression.

Finding ways to meet these needs on your own is the foundation of overcoming self-sabotage.

You are going to feel far more willing to exercise if you got a good night's sleep. You are going to feel much better about work if you don't have to sit there with an ongoing backache and instead seek out a professional who can help you with your posture or chiropractic care or massage. You are going to enjoy spending time in your home if your home is organized and meaningful to you. You are going to feel better about yourself each day if you take the time to put yourself together with care.

These things are not little things; they are big things. You just can't see it because their impact is that you do them every day.

Understanding your needs, meeting the ones you are responsible for, and then allowing yourself to show up so others can meet the ones you can't do on your own will help you break the self-sabotage cycle and build a healthier, more balanced and fulfilling life.

CHAPTER 4

BUILDING EMOTIONAL INTELLIGENCE

SELF-SABOTAGE IS ULTIMATELY JUST a product of low emotional intelligence.

To move on with our lives in a healthy, productive, and stable way, we need to understand how our brains and bodies work together. We need to understand how to interpret feelings, what different emotions mean, and what to do when we are faced with big, daunting sensations that we don't know how to handle.

We are going to specifically focus on aspects of emotional intelligence that relate to self-sabotaging behaviors, though there is an incredible body of work on EI from experts around the world that is continually growing with time.

WHAT IS EMOTIONAL INTELLIGENCE?

Emotional intelligence is the ability to understand,

interpret, and respond to your emotions in an enlightened and healthy way.

People with high emotional intelligence are often able to better get along with different types of people, feel more contentment and satisfaction in their everyday lives, and consistently take time to process and express their authentic feelings.

Mostly, though, emotional intelligence is the ability to interpret the sensations that come up in your body and understand what they are trying to tell you about your life.

The root of self-sabotage is a lack of emotional intelligence, because without the ability to understand ourselves, we inevitably become lost. These are some of the most misunderstood aspects of our brains and bodies that inevitably leave us stuck.

YOUR BRAIN IS DESIGNED TO RESIST WHAT YOU REALLY WANT

Something interesting happens in the human brain when we get what we want.

When we imagine what goals we want to achieve, we often do so with the expectation that they will elevate our quality of life in some tangible way, and once we have arrived at that place, we will be able to "coast."

"Coast" as in, let go. Relax into life. Let things be for a while.

That is not what happens.

Neurologically, when we get something we really want, we just start to want more. New research in the nature of the chemical dopamine—which was previously believed to be the driving force behind desire, lust, and acquisition—proves that it is more complex than previously thought.

In *The Molecule of More*, Daniel Z. Lieberman explains that experts who studied the hormone found that when an individual was introduced to something they highly desired, the dopamine surge would diminish after acquisition. Dopamine, it turns out, is not the chemical that gives you pleasure; it's the chemical that gives you the pleasure of wanting more.[7]

So the big, huge goal that you're working toward? You'll get there, and then there will be another mountain to scale.

This is one of the many reasons that we deeply sabotage what we truly want. We know instinctively that "arriving" won't really give us the ability to abstain from life; it will only make us hungrier for more. Sometimes, we don't feel up to that challenge.

So, while we're on the way, a toxic cocktail of neurological biases start piling up on one another, and we start to resent, judge, and even vilify the object of our greatest desire.

What happens when we start to chase what we really want: We resist doing the work that it takes to actually get it because we are so afraid of not having it, any brush with failure makes us rescind our effort and tense up.

When we go so long not having what we really want, we create subconscious associations between having it and "being bad," because we have judged others for having it.

When we get it, we fear losing it so badly that we push it away from ourselves so as to not have to withstand the pain.

We are so deeply enmeshed in the mental state of "wanting," we cannot shift to a state of "having."

First, when we want something really, really badly, it is often because we have unrealistic expectations associated with it. We imagine that it will change our lives in some formidable way, and often, that's not the case.

When we are relying on some goal or life change to "save" us in some unrealistic way, any incident of failure will trigger us to stop trying. For example: If we are absolutely certain that a romantic partner will help us stop being depressed, we are going to be extremely sensitive to rejection, because it makes us feel as though we will never get over depression.

Of course, the obvious issue here is that dating is a process of trial and error. You have to fail first to succeed.

Then, for all the time we spend not having the thing we want, such as a romantic relationship, our brains have to justify and validate our stance in life as a form of self-protection. This is why we unconsciously vilify those who do have what we want. Instead of being inspired by their success, we doubt them. We become a skeptic about relationships, being so jealous of others' happiness we assume that they must be faking it, or that love "isn't real," or that they'll split eventually, anyway.

If we hold tightly to these beliefs for long enough, guess what will happen when we finally get that relationship we really want? Of course, we are going to doubt it and assume it will also fail.

This is what's going on when people push others away or give up on their big dreams the moment something challenging comes up. When we are so scared that we are going to lose something, we tend to push it away from ourselves first as a means of self-preservation.

So let's say that you work through the limiting beliefs that are creating this much resistance in your life, and you do eventually allow yourself to build and have the thing you really, really want. Next, you'll be upon the last and most trying challenge, which is the shift from "survival mode" to "thriving mode."

If you have spent the majority of your life in a state in which you are "just getting by," you are not going to know how to adapt to a life in which you are relaxed and enjoying it. You are going to resist it, feel guilty, perhaps overspend or disregard responsibilities. You are, in your head, "balancing out" the years of difficulty with years of complete relaxation. However, this is not how it works.

When we are so deeply enmeshed in the feeling of "wanting," it becomes extremely hard to adjust to the experience of "having."

This is because any change, no matter how positive, is uncomfortable until it is also familiar.

It is difficult to acknowledge the ways in which we are so deeply inclined to self-validate, so we end up standing in our own way out of pride. It is even more difficult to acknowledge that very often, the things we envy in others are fragments of our deepest desires, the ones we won't allow ourselves to have.

Yes, your brain is predisposed to want greater things, and more of them. But by understanding its processes and tendencies, you can override the programming and start governing your own life.

YOUR BODY IS GOVERNED BY A HOMEOSTATIC IMPULSE

Your brain is built to reinforce and regulate your life.

Your subconscious mind has something called a homeostatic impulse, which regulates functions like body temperature, heartbeat, and breathing. Brian Tracy explained it like this: "Through your autonomic nervous system, [your homeostatic impulse] maintains a balance among the hundreds of chemicals in your billions of cells so that your entire physical machine functions in complete harmony most of the time."[8]

But what many people don't realize is that just as your brain is built to regulate your physical self, it tries to regulate your mental self. Your mind is constantly filtering and bringing to your attention information and stimuli that affirm your preexisting beliefs (this is known in psychology as confirmation bias) as well as presenting you with repeated thoughts and impulses that mimic and mirror what you've done in the past.

Your subconscious mind is the gatekeeper of your comfort zone.

It is also the realm in which you can either habituate yourself to expect and routinely seek the actions that would build and reinforce the greatest success, happiness, wholeness, or healing of your life.

What this teaches us is that when we are going through a healing or changing process in our lives, we have to allow our bodies to adjust to their new sense of normalcy. This is why all change, no matter how good, will be uncomfortable until it is also familiar. This is also why we can get stuck in self-destructive habits and cycles. Even though they feel good, that does not mean they are good for us.

We have to use our minds to practice discernment. We have to use our supreme intelligence to decide where we want to go, who we want to be, and then we have to allow our bodies to adjust over time.

We cannot live being governed by how we feel. Our emotions are temporary and not always reflective of reality.

YOU DON'T CHANGE IN BREAKTHROUGHS; YOU CHANGE IN MICROSHIFTS

If you're stuck in life, it's probably because you're waiting for the big bang, the breakthrough moment in which all your fears dissolve and you're overcome with clarity. The work that needs to happen happens effortlessly. Your personal transformation rips you from complacency, and you wake up to an entirely new existence.

That moment will never come.

Breakthroughs do not happen spontaneously. They are tipping points.

Revelations occur when ideas that were sitting in the margins of your mind finally get enough attention to dominate your thoughts. These are the "clicking" moments, the moments when you finally understand advice you've heard your entire life. The moments when you've habituated yourself to a pattern of behavior for long enough that it becomes instinctive.

A mind-blowing, singular breakthrough is not what changes your life. A microshift is.

Breakthroughs are what happen after hours, days, and years of the same mundane, monotonous work.

But a mind-blowing, singular breakthrough is not what changes your life. A microshift is.

As writer and media strategist Ryan Holiday has noted, epiphanies are not life-altering.[9] It's not radical moments of action that give us long-lasting, permeating change—it's the restructuring of our habits. The idea is what science philosopher Thomas Kuhn dubbed a "paradigm shift." Kuhn suggested we don't change our lives in flashes of brilliance, but through a slow process in which assumptions unravel and require new explanations. It's in these periods of flux that microshifts happen and breakthrough-level change begins to take shape.

Think of microshifts as tiny increments of change in your day-to-day life. A microshift is changing what you eat for one part of one meal just one time. Then it's doing that a second time and a third. Before you even realize what's happening, you've adopted a pattern of behavior.

What you do every single day accounts for the quality of your life and the degree of your success. It's not whether you "feel" like putting in the work, but whether or not you do it regardless.

This is because the outcomes of life are not governed by passion; they are governed by principle.

You may not think what you did this morning was important, but it was. You may not think that the little things add up, but they do. Consider the age-old brainteaser: Would you rather have $1 million in hand today or a penny that doubles in value every day for the next month? The $1 million right now sounds great, but after a 31-day month, that one penny would be worth over $10 million.

Making big, sweeping changes is not difficult because we are flawed, incompetent beings. It's difficult because we are not meant to live outside of our comfort zones.

If you want to change your life, you need to make tiny, nearly undetectable decisions every hour of every day until those choices are habituated. Then you'll just continue to do them.

If you want to spend less time on your phone, deny yourself the chance to check it one time today. If you want to eat healthier, drink half a cup of water today. If you want to sleep more, go to bed 10 minutes earlier tonight than you did last night.

If you want to exercise more, do it now for just 10 minutes. If you want to read, read one page. If you want to meditate, do so for 30 seconds.

Then keep doing those things. Do them every single day. You'll get used to not checking your phone. You'll want more water, and you'll drink more water. You'll run for 10 minutes, and you won't feel like you have to stop, so you won't. You'll read one page, grow interested, and read another.

At our most instinctive, physiological level, "change" translates to something dangerous and potentially life-threatening. No wonder why we build our own cages and stay in them, even though there's no lock on the door.

Trying to shock yourself into a new life isn't going to work, and that's why it hasn't yet.

You don't need to wait until you feel like changing to start changing. All you need is to make one microshift at a time and then let the energy and momentum build.

YOUR MIND IS ANTIFRAGILE

Is your brain the greatest antagonist in your life?

Is irrational fear at the core of the majority of your greatest stressors?

Do you ever have the hunch that you're almost seeking out problems, creating issues where they don't exist, overreacting, overthinking, and catastrophizing?

If you said "yes" to these, congratulations, you're self-aware.

You're also just like anybody else.

If you feel like you're always subconsciously scanning your life trying to identify the next thing to worry about, the next potential threat to fear, you'd be right.

What we fear most is what our minds identify as the least likely threat that we cannot control. If the threat is highly likely, we don't fear it—we respond to it. That's why most worry comes from not just identifying the one thing we cannot control, but the one small, unlikely thing we cannot control.

So why do our minds need this, though?

Can't we just enjoy what we have and be grateful?

To a point, absolutely.

But our minds also need adversity, and that's why it's instinctual to keep creating problems—even if there aren't any real ones in front of us.

The human mind is something called antifragile, which

means that it actually gets better with adversity. Like a rock that becomes a diamond under pressure or an immune system that strengthens after repeated exposure to germs, the mind requires stimulation in the form of a challenge.

If you deny and reject any kind of real challenge in your life, your brain will compensate by creating a problem to overcome. Except this time, there won't be any reward at the end. It will just be you battling you for the rest of your life.

The cultural obsession with chasing happiness, shielding oneself from anything triggering, and the idea that life is primarily "good" and any challenge we face is a mistake of fate are what actually weaken us mentally.

Shielding the mind from any adversity makes us more vulnerable to anxiety, panic, and chaos.

Those who can't help but create problems in their minds often do so because they have ceased creative control of their existence. They move into the passenger's seat, thinking that life happens to them, rather than being a product of their actions.

Who wouldn't be afraid if that were the case?

But what most people don't tell you is that adversity makes you creative. It activates a part of you that is often latent.

It makes things interesting. Part of the human narrative is wanting something to overcome.

The trick is keeping it in balance. Choosing to exit your comfort zone and endure pain for a worthy cause.

Focusing on problems that are real problems in the world, like hunger or politics or whatever else.

But most importantly, it's about staying engaged with what we can control in life, which is most things if you really think about it. Antifragile things need tension, resistance, adversity, and pain to break and transform. We get this by deeply communing with life and being part of it, rather than fearing our emotions and sitting on the sidelines.

You can't stay there forever, nor do you really want to. Embracing the grit of it all was what you were made for. Lean in and start living.

NEW CHANGE CREATES ADJUSTMENT SHOCK

Of all the things that nobody tells you about life, that you might not experience instantaneous happiness after a positive life change is perhaps the most confusing.

The truth about your psyche is this: Anything that is new,

even if it is good, will feel uncomfortable until it is also familiar.

Our brain works the opposite way, too, in that whatever is familiar is what we perceive to be good and comfortable, even if those behaviors, habits, or relationships are actually toxic or destructive.

Positive life events can actually trigger depressive episodes. This happens for a few reasons: First, a spike and then decline in mood or attitude can exacerbate stress. Second, the expectation that a positive event will eliminate all stress and bring unprecedented happiness is a destructive one, because the event rarely does that. This is why weddings, childbirth, or a new job can be so incredibly stressful. On top of being a massive life change, there's also the silent assumption that this should be a wholly positive thing, and anxiety and tension should be eliminated.

It is jarring to discover this isn't the case.

Overall, it comes down to the simple fact that any accomplishments, achievements, or life changes, no matter how positive, elicit change. Change elicits stress. This is particularly true for those who are already predisposed to anxiety and depression, because the concept of one's comfort zone is absolutely essential to stabilizing their mood. This is also why those people can often seem overwhelmingly particular or narrow-minded.

WHAT ARE THE SIGNS OF ADJUSTMENT SHOCK?

Adjustment shock can manifest as simply an increase in anxiety or irritability. However, it is often more complex than that.

Adjustment shock often comes across as hypervigilance. If you make financial gains, your mind immediately shifts to what could potentially derail your progress, a big bill that could come up, or the loss of the job you just got. If you have a new, happy relationship, you could become paranoid about infidelity or lies.

Adjustment shock can bring to light unconscious attachments and beliefs. If you are someone who was raised to think that wealthy people are morally corrupt, you are going to resist having more money. If you wanted to be famous to be more loved, you are going to resist public success, because "famous" people are often more criticized and disliked than the average person.

Adjustment shock can bring feelings of intense fear. This is because when we attain something we very much care about or have worked toward for a long time, our instinct can be to shield ourselves from the potential loss of it by putting up walls and desensitizing ourselves to the experience.

We often resist most deeply the things that we want most.

This is because of adjustment shock, though we don't always know that's what's causing the resistance.

It is scary to receive everything we want, because it forces us to shift out of a survivalist, fear-based mindset and into a more stabilized one. If all we are accustomed to is doing what we need to do to survive, we are then confronted with the next phases of our self-actualization.

If we are no longer worried about basic survival, our minds are free to turn to the bigger questions in life: What is our purpose? Have we lived meaningfully? Are we who we want to be?

We often think of big achievements as a "get out of life easier" card. They rarely are that. In fact, the opposite tends to happen. They level us up, force us into greater responsibilities, to think more deeply about big issues, to question ourselves and what we previously knew to be true.

Big achievements actually pressure us to become increasingly better versions of ourselves. This is a net positive for our lives but can be just as uncomfortable as struggling was, if not more so.

HOW DO I OVERCOME ADJUSTMENT SHOCK?

When something positive happens in your life, you are going to have to adjust your mindset about other things to create alignment and a new, more accurate and sustainable perspective.

If you have anxiety about having more money, you will need to learn how to manage it better. If you have anxiety about relationships, you will need to learn to relate to others like you never have before.

Your big life change is going to force you to level up in every way imaginable, and the way to overcome the initial fear of stepping into the unknown is to familiarize yourself with it, to make it a part of you, one that you are certain you are prepared for—and that you deserve.

PSYCHIC THINKING ISN'T WISDOM

When we talk about "psychic thinking," we are not referring to the palm-reading, neon-sign-advertised occultist professionals you can hire to evaluate your energy and predict your future.

Psychic thinking is far more insidious than that.

Psychic thinking is assuming you know what somebody else is thinking or what they intend to do. It is assuming that the least likely outcome is the most viable outcome, because you feel it most strongly. It is believing that you have missed out on "another life," a path you did not choose, that you were possibly more meant for. It is believing that the person with whom you have the most electric connection is your most ideal life partner.

Of course, the way other people see us is dynamic. Their thoughts, feelings, and intentions are largely if not entirely unknown to us. The least likely outcome is just that: the least likely outcome. There is no such thing as the path we could have taken, only a projection of our needs and desires onto another fantastical idea of what our lives might be. Electric connection is not soulmateship; love and compatibility are not the same thing.

Psychic thinking detaches us from reality. In place of logic, we put emotions, ones that are often incorrect, unreliable, and wholly biased toward what we want to believe.

Beyond being inconveniencing, psychic thinking is absolutely terrible for your mental health. Psychic thinking breeds anxiety and depression. It's not just that something scares or upsets us; it's that we believe that the thought must not only be real, but predictive of future events. Instead of feeling like we are having a down day, psychic thinking makes us assume we are having a terrible life.

We heard "trust yourself" and then began to liken ourselves to oracles, that when a particularly triggering thought or feeling passes through us, it must indicate something more to come.

Indeed, psychic thinking as a whole has begun taking on an entirely new light because of the popularity of pop psychology, dating back to the 50s and 60s. Trust yourself, the gurus tell you. Deep down, you know the truth.

This is valid. Your intestines are literally connected to the stem of your brain; the bacteria in your stomach respond to subconscious intelligent awareness faster than your mind can. This is why your "gut" is indeed correct on instinct. But when this advice is given to people who cannot differentiate a gut feeling from fear or from a passing thought that has no bearing on reality or their lives as a whole, it becomes a dangerous practice in which they become completely stuck and limited because they assume their random feelings are all real—and then not only real, but a prediction for what's to come.

Psychic thinking is nothing more than a series of cognitive biases, the most prominent of which are the following:

CONFIRMATION

At any moment in time, your brain is inundated with stimuli. To help you process, your conscious mind is aware of about 10% of it or less. Your subconscious mind is still paying attention, logging away information you might one day need.

However, what determines what makes it to that 10% of our conscious awareness has a lot to do with what we already believe. Our brains are literally working to filter out information that does not support our preexisting ideas, and then to draw our attention to information that does. This means that we are subject to a "confirmation bias," which is that we literally seek out and sort through stimuli that supports what we want to think.

EXTRAPOLATION

Extrapolation is when we take our current circumstances and then project them out into the future. Ryan Holiday says it best: "This moment is not my life. It is a moment in my life."

Extrapolation makes us think that we are the sum of our past or current experiences, that whatever stressors or anxieties we are currently experiencing are ones that we will grapple with for the rest of our lives. Unable to see through the problem at hand, we assume it will never resolve itself. Unfortunately, this can become a self-fulfilling prophecy. If we are so easily defeated and exhausted by the idea that we will never get over our problems, then we make it more likely that we will hang onto them instead of logically trying to resolve them, for a lot more time than is necessary.

SPOTLIGHTING

Everyone thinks that the world revolves around them. You are thinking about you and your own interests all day, every day. It can be challenging to forget that others are not thinking about us with such intensity; they are thinking about themselves.

The spotlight effect is what happens when we imagine that our lives are performative, or "on display" for others to consume. We remember the last two or three embarrassing things we have done and imagine that others are thinking about them actively as well. Can you recall the last two or three embarrassing things someone else did? Of course you can't. Because you aren't paying attention.

Spotlighting gives us the false impression that the world is all about us, when it is not.

These biases plus others, when combined with psychic thinking, or the idea that our assumptions and feelings about the world will transpose into reality, are harmful and mostly incorrect. Instead of trying to predict what will happen next, our energy is better used when it's focused intently on the moment—the infinite "now," the mystics would say—because the truth is that the past and future are illusions in the present, and all we have is the present.

Instead of trying to use your intelligence to hack what's next, try to get better at where you are currently. That's what's really going to change the outcomes of your life.

LOGICAL LAPSES ARE GIVING YOU PROFOUND ANXIETY

Most of the anxiety you experience in life is the result in inefficient critical-thinking skills. You might assume that because you are anxious, you are an overthinker, someone who obsesses about unlikely and scary outcomes more than is reasonable. The reality is that you are an under-thinker.

You're missing a part of your reasoning process.

Let's start at the beginning. Anxiety is a normal emotion that every person experiences at some point in their lives, typically when circumstances are stressful, tense, or scary. When anxiety is chronic and begins to interfere with day-to-day functioning, it becomes a clinical disorder.

We understand the importance of speaking about mental health with the same degree of legitimacy as physical health. However, in the same way that we'd question what someone keeps tripping over if they repeatedly sprain their ankle, a lot of anxiety is similarly circumstantial, as many illnesses are. Specifically, anxiety tends to be the result of an inability to process acutely stressful and ongoing circumstances.

If we want to heal, we have to learn to process.

This applies to everyone, not just those with a diagnosis.

One of the hallmarks of anxiety is rapid thinking. Because you are focusing on some issue so deeply and for so much time, you assume that you are also thinking through the issue thoroughly and arriving at the most likely conclusion. However, the opposite is happening.

You're experiencing a logical lapse. You're jumping to the worst-case scenario because you aren't thinking clearly, and then you are engaging your fight-or-flight response because the worst-case scenario makes you feel threatened. This is why you obsess about that one, terrifying idea. Your body is responding as though it's an immediate threat, and until you "defeat" or overcome it, your body will do its job, which is to keep you in defense mode, which is really a heightened state of awareness to the "enemy."

WHAT IS A LOGICAL LAPSE?

Think of something that you aren't afraid of, maybe something that other people might find scary.

Maybe you aren't afraid of flying in an airplane. Many people are. Maybe you aren't afraid of being single. Many people are. Maybe you aren't afraid of commitment. Many people are. Surely you can think of at least one thing in your life that you are truly unafraid of.

Why aren't you afraid of it? Because you don't have a logical lapse there.

You can visualize yourself going on an airplane and successfully getting off without freaking out. You can visualize yourself being happily single or happily committed. Even if the worst were to happen, you can think a situation through in its entirety, from exposition to climax to conclusion. You know what you would do. You have a plan.

When you experience a logical lapse, the climax becomes the conclusion. You imagine a situation, you figure that you would panic, and then because you're scared, you never think through the rest of the scenario. You never think about how you'd get through it, what you'd do to respond, and how you'd eventually move on with your life afterwards. If you were able to do this, you wouldn't be scared of it, because you wouldn't think it had the power to "end" you.

This is why exposure is the most common treatment for irrational fear. By reintroducing the stressor into your life in a safe way, you are able to reestablish a line of thinking that is healthier and calmer. Basically, you prove to yourself that you will be okay, even if something scary does happen (which most of the time it does not).

Either way, mental strength is not just hoping that nothing ever goes wrong. It is believing that we have the capacity to handle it if it does.

Maybe you don't have that self-belief yet. That's okay. It's not something you're born with; it's something you build slowly and over time. It's something you develop with practice, by addressing small problems, and then learning healthy coping mechanisms and effective reasoning skills.

The thing is that there are millions of scary things that can happen to us in our lives. That is true for everyone. When we are hung up on one scary thing over another, it's not because it's a more imminent or likely threat; it's because we are less convinced we would be able to respond to it.

To heal, we don't need to avoid it. We need to develop logic to see situations for what they are and respond appropriately to them.

So often in life, our biggest anxiety comes not from what's actually happening, but how we think about what is happening. In that, we reclaim our emotional freedom and power.

FAULTY INFERENCES ARE HOLDING YOU BACK FROM SUCCESS

If you're familiar with body typing, you'll probably be familiar with the terms endomorph, mesomorph, and ectomorph. Though everyone actually falls somewhere within the spectrum of these (meaning that everyone has varying degrees of each), the traits you default to are typically your primary body type.[10]

If you've studied these types, you'll know that endomorphic bodies are often associated with increased fat retention. The assumption here is that these people have the worst metabolisms, but that is false. Endomorphs actually have the best metabolisms of anyone. They are alive today because their ancestors adequately adapted to survive. Their metabolisms do precisely what they were intended to do: store fat for later use.

Something similar happens with highly intelligent people who experience high levels of anxiety. You assume that because these people are smart, they would be able to use logic to disrupt illogical fears. (Logical lapses, or an inability to adequately reason, often generate anxiety.)

However, their brains are doing exactly what they were meant to do, which is to piece together unrelated stimuli and identify potential threats.

Highly intelligent people have a psychological function others do not, which is the ability to infer. They can extract meaning and understanding from things that others simply take at face value. This is why people who have extremely high IQs often struggle with basic things such as social skills or driving a car. Where others see the world as one-dimensional, the highly intelligent see it as three-dimensional. They think more deeply than is often necessary. This gives them their ability to create, understand, strategize, and invent.

In the same way that the endomorph's excellent metabolism can work against them, so too can a highly intelligent person's brain. This is because at times, they make something called "faulty inferences," which are when fallacies, biases, and incorrect assumptions are made from valid evidence.

What's happening in your brain when you're very anxious is that you're taking an often innocuous stimulus and extracting some kind of meaning or prediction from it. When you're scared, your brain is working in overdrive to identify the thing that can potentially hurt you and then creatively come up with ways to completely avoid that experience. The smarter you are, the better you become at this.

However, the more you avoid a fear, the more intense it becomes.

WHAT'S A FAULTY INFERENCE?

A faulty inference is when you come up with a false conclusion based on valid evidence.

This means that what you're seeing, experiencing, or understanding might be real, but the assumptions that you are piecing together from it are either not real or are highly unlikely.

One example is a hasty generalization, which is when you make a claim about an entire group of people based on one or two experiences you've had. This is the bias at the base of a lot of racism and prejudice. Another example is *post hoc ergo propter hoc*, which is what happens when you assume that because two things happened around the same time, they must be related, even if they aren't.

A false dichotomy happens when you assume that there are only two possibilities that could be valid, when in reality, there are far more that you simply aren't aware of. An example of this is when your boss calls you to a private meeting, and you assume you must either be getting a promotion or getting fired. A slippery slope, to play off of that example, is another false inference in which you assume that one event will set off a series of others, even if they certainly will not.

These are just some of the myriad ways your brain can, in a sense, betray you. Though it intends to keep you alert and aware, sometimes, the threat becomes overinflated. Unable to decipher the difference, your body responds regardless.

HOW DO I CORRECT THIS?

Correcting faulty inferencing begins with first being aware that you're doing it. In the majority of cases, once you realize that you're thinking in a false dichotomy or making a hasty generalization, you stop doing it. You understand what it is, and you let it go.

Training your brain to stop doing it automatically takes time. Think of your mind like a search engine that autofills your terms. If it's something you've input many times over the years, it's still going to come up for a while. You have to work on consistently adding new thoughts, options, and stimuli to shift what it comes up with naturally.

This is not only possible; it's inevitable. What you consistently do is what you adapt to. Your brain will start to reorient your comfort zone, and eventually it will feel as natural to think logically as it once did to think dramatically. It will feel as natural to be calm as it does now to feel anxious. It takes awareness, and it takes time. But it is always possible.

WORRYING IS THE WEAKEST DEFENSE SYSTEM

Rumination is the birthplace of creativity. They're controlled by the same part of the brain.[11]

That's the neurological reason there's a stereotype about "depressed creatives." Any artist will tell you that the toughest times in their lives inspired the most groundbreaking work. What they won't tell you, though, is that crisis is not necessary to function.

Well, of course it's not, you're thinking. Crisis is the worst-case scenario. And yet how many of us place ourselves in a state of panic over fear of that "least likely scenario" coming true? How many of us, in an effort to shield ourselves from panic, actually create a crisis out of our fear each day?

We're not just masochists. We're wildly intelligent unconsciously functioning beings. Our brains understand something: If we imagine our worst fears, we can prepare for them. If we mull them over again and again, we can feel protected in a way. If we are ready for the storm, it can't hurt us.

Except it can.

Worrying excessively is not a malfunction. You are not of lesser character because you can't "just stop" and "enjoy life." Worrying is a subconscious defense mechanism. It's what we do when we care about something so much we are equally terrified that it could hurt us, so we prepare to fight for it.

What is the exact opposite of your fear? That's what you want. That's what you want so much that you'd go to the ends of your sanity to defend it.

There's nothing wrong with you for thinking this way, but there's also nothing wrong with you for being ready to move in a new direction.

The reality is that worrying does not protect us in the way that we think it might. We cannot beat fear to the finish line. Worrying sensitizes us to an infinity of negative possible outcomes. It shifts our mindset to expect, seek out, and create a worst-case scenario. If a crisis were to occur, we'd start panicking, because our brains and bodies had been preparing for this epic war for a long time.

Had we not premeditated these fears so excessively, we wouldn't be as impacted were they to actually happen. We'd see the situation for what it is and respond accordingly.

That's where the nasty cycle forms: Once we worry ourselves sick over something that is totally delusional, and it doesn't happen—because, of course, it was never going to—we start to associate worry with safety. See? I thought this through so many times that I've avoided it.

But that's not what's happening at all.

Just telling someone to stop worrying and be present strengthens their impulse to be fearful, because you are effectively asking them to place their guards down. Making yourself feel more vulnerable when you're already at your edge is not the answer.

Instead, you have to find a different way to feel safe.

Rather than spending your time rehearsing how much you'd panic if such-and-such a situation were to come to fruition, imagine how a third party would handle it if they were in your shoes. Imagine getting to the other side of the issue, perhaps even treating it as an opportunity to create something you otherwise couldn't.

Rather than spending your time shrinking yourself and your life out of fear of potentially confronting some kind of hardship, work on developing your self-esteem and know that even if you were to fail, you wouldn't be judged, exiled, or hated in the way you fear.

Rather than spending your life trying to identify the next thing to worry about and then "overcome," learn to move into a new pattern of thinking in which you recognize that you don't need to balance out the bad with the good to live a full and fair life. Stability and wholeness, health and vitality are your birthright. You are allowed to have everything you want. You are permitted to be at peace.

Worrying is so primal in the way that it fulfills a deep need within us to feel as though we've conquered, and thus are protected and saved. Yet at the same time, our discomfort with it is a higher aspect of ourselves informing us that it isn't necessary, and in fact, it's holding us back from the people we want and are meant to be.

There's a better way to feed your emotional hunger, and it's not fighting yourself for your own inner peace.

CHAPTER 5

RELEASING THE PAST

THROUGHOUT THE COURSE of our lives, we will routinely go through a process of self-reinvention.

Over time, we are meant to change, and we are designed to evolve. Our bodies show us this as we eliminate and replace cells to the point that some argue we are essentially completely made "new" again every seven years.[12]

Our mental and emotional growth follow a similar process, though it tends to occur much more often. It makes sense, then, that some of our most profound suffering comes from resistance to this natural process. We are in pain because though we must change our lives, we are holding onto baggage and debris from the past. As we carry unresolved emotions from day to day, we gradually move our past trauma into our future lives.

Releasing the past is a process, and a practice—one that we have to learn. This is where we begin.

HOW TO START LETTING GO

You cannot force yourself to let go, no matter how much you know you want to.

Right now, you are being called to release your old self: your prior afflictions, past relationships, and all of the guilt from the time you spent denying yourself what you really wanted and needed out of life. Recovering from self-sabotage always necessitates a process of letting go.

However, you cannot force something out of your brain space, no matter how much you don't want it to be there.

You cannot simply loosen your grip, relax a little, and will yourself to stop thinking entirely about something around which your entire world used to orbit.

This is not how it goes.

You are not going to let go the moment someone tells you to "move on," the day you realize you have to admit certain defeat, the heart-dropping second it occurs to you that hope is, indeed, futile.

You do not let go by simply willing yourself not to care anymore. This is something that people who have never been really, really hung up on something would assume. This is something that people who have never been deeply attached to something for a sense of safety and security and love and their future believe.

There is nothing wrong with you because you almost get angry when people tell you to just "let go" so nonchalantly, as though they couldn't fathom the storms in your head and heart.

How can you become so passive about something you have spent so much of your time in your life actively working to maintain and then restore?

You can't, and you don't.

You start to let go on the day you take one step toward building a new life and then let yourself lie in bed and stare at the ceiling and cry for as many hours as you need.

You start to let go on the day you realize that you cannot continue to revolve around a missing gap in your life, and going on as you were before will simply not be an option.

You start to let go at the moment you realize that this is the impetus, this is the catalyst, this is that moment the movies are made about and the books are written around and songs are inspired by.

This is the moment you realize that you will never find peace standing in the ruins of what you used to be.

You can only move on if you start building something new.

You let go when you build a new life so immersive and engaging and exciting, you slowly, over time, forget about the past.

When we try to force ourselves to "let go" of something, we grip onto it tighter, and harder, and more passionately than ever before. It's like if someone tells you to not think of a white elephant, that's the only thing you'll be able to focus on.

Our hearts work the same way as our minds in this regard. As long as we are telling ourselves that we must let go, the more deeply we feel attached.

So don't tell yourself to let go.

Instead, tell yourself that you can cry for as long as you need. That you can fall to pieces and be a mess and let your life collapse and crumble. Tell yourself that you can let your foundation fall through.

What you will realize is that you are still standing.

What you build in the wake and the aftermath of loss will be so profound, so stunning, you will realize that maybe the loss was part of the plan. Maybe it awakened a part of you that would have remained dormant had you not been pushed the way you were.

If you are certain that you cannot let go of what is hurting you, then don't.

But take one step today, and another tomorrow, to rebuild a new life for yourself. Piece by piece, day by day.

Because sooner or later, you're going to go an hour and realize you didn't think about them or it. Then a day, then a week...and then years and swaths of your life drift by and everything you thought would break you becomes a distant memory, something you look back at and smile.

Everything you lose becomes something you are profoundly grateful for. With time, you see that it was not the path. It was what was standing in your way.

THE PSYCHOLOGICAL TRICK TO RELEASE OLD EXPERIENCES

Just because an experience has ended doesn't mean it's over.

We store unfinished and unresolved emotional experiences within our bodies. Cognitively, we often find that we are stunted by the time in our lives in which we were damaged or traumatized. We got scared, we never got over the fear, and as a result, we stopped growing.

Often what we don't realize is that the experiences that hurt us most aren't usually the ones that we are indifferent about: There is something within them that we deeply wanted or still desire. We weren't broken by a breakup; we were broken by wanting love that wasn't right for us. We weren't devastated by a loss; we were devastated because we wanted, so badly, for that person or thing to remain in our lives.

We mentally become trapped in these places from which we still crave an experience. What we don't realize is that we have to sort of free ourselves from it so that we can go forth and create it in real time.

Instead of accepting the ways we think life did not work out, we have to be able to see what was at the core of our desire and figure out a way to still give ourselves that experience now.

If you truly want to let go of a past experience, you have to reenter it through your memory. Close your eyes and find the feeling in your body that is uncomfortable.

This is your portal to its root. Follow the feeling and ask it to show you where it started. You'll remember a time, place, or experience. Sometimes, the memory is fresh enough that you don't need to do this, and you can simply reenter the memory by imagining that you are back where it all began.

Now what you have to do is to superimpose a narrative to your younger self. You need to imagine that you, your healed and happy older self, is imparting some wisdom.

Imagine sitting next to your younger self as they got their heart broken and giving them very specific instructions about why this is absolutely for the best and although they cannot know it yet, there is another relationship out there that is far, far better.

Imagine sitting next to your younger self when they felt really down and giving them the exact instructions regarding what they need to do to feel better: who they need to call, where they need to go, what they need to begin doing, and what they need to stop doing.

Most importantly, imagine telling your younger self that absolutely everything—yes, everything—is going to be okay. That their fears are largely unfounded, that good things are coming, and that life will turn out well in the end.

You have to do this to release the old attachment and allow that part of yourself to reattach to the present moment and what exists within it.

Though you cannot change what happened in the past, by shifting your perspective of it, you can change how you are right now. You can change the story, and you can change your life. You can stop holding onto the old life in which you were required to be someone you inherently are not.

The truth is that when we are unhealthily attached to something in the past, our perspective of it is often distorted. We aren't seeing reality for what it was, and we need to assist ourselves in being able to broaden our mindset and open up to the truth. Instead of longing for what we didn't get then, we have to release ourselves from the past and start putting our energy into building that experience right now.

When we do this, we become free to step into the field of infinite potential. We become free to be who we always wanted, to create what we always wanted, and to have what we always wanted. The time is now, and the place is here.

Ruminating over the past doesn't mean you want to return to it.

Not being able to forget what happened doesn't mean you're content to keep reliving it again and again, even though right now, you very much are.

The wildest thing about life is how unassumingly it keeps moving. You lose the person closest to you and the world affords you a few days of grieving, and then you're expected to just keep going. You go through something so life-shifting, mind-altering, and deeply traumatic, then find that society only has a small bandwidth for tolerating your fear.

Here's what you're allowed: You're okay to cry and you're forgiven for being sad or canceling a few plans here and there. You're permitted a few days off of work and someone to listen to you vent a handful of times.

But processing and accepting the gravity of something that touched every last inch of you is not something you can do on a mental-health day. It's not something the world affords you enough time for, and so you botch the job. You carry on.

One day, you wake up and discover that by every identifiable measure, you have moved on. You're so many miles from where you started, you can't even remember it clearly. What you're underestimating is the fact that though you can leave a place, or a person, or a situation...you can't leave yourself.

Why would it ever come as a surprise that you keep thinking about the past? You weren't given the opportunity to shine a light on that particular darkness and deem it okay. You weren't given much of anything at all.

When your mind is stuck in the past, it isn't because it wants to return there; it's because you were impacted far more deeply than you ever realized, and the aftershocks are still rippling through you.

They surface as thoughts here and there, but under the surface is a deep echo that has the power to place you right back where you were as though you never left.

You can leave the country, get remarried, build a whole new career, date 12 other people, find an entirely new friend group, feel happier and more fulfilled than ever, and still grieve for what your younger self went through.

Even though you're different on the outside, that part of you still very much exists within. That younger self doesn't just want you to keep walking; it wants you to turn around and acknowledge it.

You will, with time.

You are not wrong or broken for feeling the way that you do. You responded to your circumstances as any healthy person would have. If anyone else was in your shoes, they would have reacted the exact same way. They would feel the exact same way.

You were a healthy person who went through something traumatic and responded accordingly.

You are someone who moved on because they had to, but who wasn't sick enough to disassociate entirely from the past.

The fact that you can still recall what happened is a signal that you're healthier than you think, more willing to heal than you realize, and more forgiving than you ever imagined you could be. Everything that's haunted you is rising in your consciousness so you can see it and bow out with grace.

You are not the person you were, even if all those pieces are still very much a part of you.

You are not broken for being in pain; you're seeing yourself out of it.

LETTING GO OF UNREALISTIC EXPECTATIONS

It is not that brave to say you love your body only after you've contorted it to precisely what you want it to look like.

It is not that brave to say you don't care about possessions when you have access to everything in the world.

It is not that brave to say you aren't motivated by money when you have enough of it.

When you only find happiness and peace after you've fixed every flaw, mastered every challenge, and are living decidedly in the "after" part of the picture of your life, you have not resolved anything.

You have only reinforced the idea that you cannot be okay until everything is perfect.

The truth is that you do not change your life when you fix every piece and call that healing.

You change your life when you start showing up exactly as you are. You change your life when you become comfortable with being happy here, even if you want to go forward. You change your life when you can love yourself even though you don't look exactly the way you want to. You change your life when you are principled about money and love and relationships, when you treat strangers as well as you do your CEO, and when you manage $1,000 the same way you would $10,000.

You change your life when you start doing the truly scary thing, which is showing up exactly as you are.

Most of the problems that exist in our lives are distractions from the real problem, which is that we are not comfortable in the present moment, as we are, here and now.

So we must heal that first. We must address that initially. Because everything else builds from it.

We must be brave and confront our discomfort, sit with it even if it churns our stomachs and pinches our faces and makes us certain we will never find a way out. (We will.)

We must listen to what's wrong, feel it, move through it, allow it to be.

The truth is that this discomfort is the true problem, and we are running around trying to fix one thing after another because those are all just symptoms.

If we become okay with money, we're onto our bodies. If we're okay with our bodies, we're onto our relationships. Once we master all the things we care about, we start at the beginning, we try to level up, to change, to fix, to identify a problem that is any problem but the actual problem at hand.

When you start showing up as exactly who you are, you start radically changing your life.

You start receiving authentic love. You start doing your best and most profitable and effortless work. You start laughing; you start enjoying things again. You start realizing that you just needed anything to project all this fear onto, so you chose the most vulnerable and common issues in life.

When you start showing up exactly as you are, you cut the bullshit.

You declare to the world that you will not only love yourself when it sees you as worthy.

You will not only have values when you have everything you could ever need.

You will not only be principled once you get where you want to be.

You will not only be happy once someone loves you.

When you show up as you are, you disrupt this pattern.

The goodness of life is no longer reserved for some version of you that you'll probably never be.

This was always a game for you to explain to yourself why

it is you didn't feel good naturally, before you knew how to start showing up and allowing your feelings. When you still lived in the darkness, you had to suppress that and project it onto other issues. No longer.

You are showing up as you are today and taking what's yours, not what belongs to some imaginary version of yourself. Not what you think the world thinks you're worthy of. You, here, now.

That is the true healing.

In fact, the universe does not allow perfection. Without breaks and gaps, there would be no growth. Nature depends on imperfection. Fault lines make mountains, star implosions become supernovas, and the death of one season creates the rebirth of the next.

You are not here to live up to the exact expectation that you've mustered up in your head. You are not here to do everything precisely right and precisely on time. To do so would require stripping your life of spontaneity, curiosity, and awe.

WHAT LEAVES THE PATH IS CLEARING THE PATH

There is nothing that you can do to win someone or something that is not meant to be yours.

You can fight with everything you have. You can hold on for as long as you can. You can force yourself into mental gymnastics to pick apart signs. You can have your friends read into texts and emails. You can decide that you know what's best for you and right for you. Mostly, you can wait.

You can wait forever.

What isn't right for you will never remain in your life.

There is no job, person, or city that you can force to be right for you if it is not, though you can pretend for a while. You can play games with yourself, you can justify and make ultimatums. You can say you'll try just a little longer, and you can make excuses for why things aren't working out right now.

The truth is that what is right for you will come to you and stay with you and won't stray from you for long. The truth is that when something is right for you, it brings you clarity, and when something is wrong for you, it brings you confusion.

You get stuck when you try to make something that's wrong for you right. When you try to force it into a place in your life in which it doesn't belong. You get split; you breed this internal conflict which you cannot resolve. The more it intensifies, the more you mistake it for passion. How could you ever feel so strongly about something that isn't right?

You can, because you can use your mind to get attached. You can fall in love with potential as opposed to reality. You can orchestrate and choreograph dances of how you'll live out your days when things finally settle into their rightful place. You can hinge on a fantasy life in which everything you think you want has taken root in your everyday life.

But if it isn't showing up, it's just that—a fantasy. And when we start to deeply believe in an illusion, it becomes a delusion. And a delusion can be a really compelling thing.

The truth is that what is not right for you will never remain with you. Though you might want to pretend that you don't know if this is the case, you do. You can feel it. It's why you have to grip so hard and with so little give. The things that are right for you can be free from you. You don't have to convince them that they are right. You don't have to line up the evidence as though you're pleading your case.

Sometimes, we get lost in old dreams. We get lost in the lives others wanted us to have. We get stuck on what we thought we should be, what we assumed we would have. We get derailed by all the ideas floating around our heads about what it *could* be and *should* be if only things were different, if only everything would click.

That's why life gives us this kind of insurance. Sometimes, it pulls away from us what is wrong for us when we are not willing to see it for ourselves.

Because the truth is that we do not want what is not right for us; we are simply attached to it. We are simply afraid. We are simply stuck in the assumption that nothing better will replace it, that its absence will open up a well of endless, infinite suffering for which there will be no solution. We do not want what is not right for us; we are just scared to let go of what we believe will make us secure.

The funny part is there is nothing that makes us more insecure than hanging around what isn't right for us. There's nothing that will collapse faster. There's nothing that will bring us inner turmoil quite like it.

What is not right for you will never remain in your life, and not because there are forces beyond us navigating the minutiae of our everyday lives. What is not right for you will not remain with you because deep down, you know it's not right. You are the one who eventually lets go, sees reality, and walks away. You are the one resisting, you are the one holding back, you are the one concocting healing fantasies about how great it will be when you force something wrong to finally be right.

What is not right for you does not remain with you because you don't want it, and so you don't choose it. You step away when you are ready, you let go when you are able, and you realize, all along, that all you were really in love with was a little trick of the light that made you feel safe.

RECOVERING FROM EMOTIONAL TRAUMA

You might think trauma is in your head in the metaphorical sense. It is actually in your body in the literal sense.

Trauma is what happens when something scares you and you do not get over that fear. If you do not resolve or "defeat" it, you get into, and remain in, a sustained state of fight-or-flight, which is essentially the human panic response for survival.

Trauma is the experience of disconnecting from a fundamental feeling of safety. Unless you are able to reestablish that connection, a particularly destructive bias distorts your worldview: You become hypersensitive, which means that you will ascribe intent, overthink, overreact, become triggered by innocuous stimuli, personalize neutral situations, and remain in a mental "combat mode."

After experiencing trauma, your brain will rewire itself temporarily to seek out the potential "threat" in anything, which makes it very difficult to both move on from the initial problem and then not to develop a victim complex. After all, your brain is literally trying to show you every imaginable way the world could be "out to get you."

This is why exposure is so effective as a treatment for fear or anxiety. By gradually reintroducing the stressor into someone's life—and showing them that they are able to handle it—the brain is able to return to a neutral state because a feeling of control and security is being reestablished.

This is also why people who have stronger social ties and mental resilience prior to a traumatic event are more likely to use the event as a catalyst for self-reflection, growth, compassion, and healing as opposed to self-destruction. They had multiple ties to that essential feeling of "safety," so even if one was eroded or severed, others still were there to support them.

What happens to your brain after a traumatic event?

Neurologically, we process stress in three parts of the brain.[13]

The first is the amygdala, the second is the hippocampus, and the third is the prefrontal cortex. Individuals suffering from post-traumatic stress disorder (PTSD) have a smaller hippocampus (the center of emotion and memory), increased amygdala function (the center of rumination and creativity), and decreased medial prefrontal/anterior cingulate function (the center that governs complex behaviors like planning and self-development).

It becomes clear, then, why trauma tends to have the following impact on us:

- Our brains stop processing memory fully, leaving us with fragments of what happened, sometimes contributing to the feeling of disassociation.

- Our ability to manage a range of emotions decreases.
- We become stifled and stuck, have trouble planning for the future, and our self-development and actualization come to a halt.
- When we enter a state of fight-or-flight, our body literally ceases any advanced function that is not necessary for our survival. The body's main receptors become extremely sensitive and reactive to stimuli. This is a beautiful and essential part of being human; it's kept us alive as a species. However, it is not a state that is meant to be sustained.

Centuries ago, when we were at the lower rung of actualization, or the bottom of Maslow's hierarchy,[14] what concerned us most was physical survival. Today, our focus is primarily on self-actualization and meaningfulness and trying to feel "safe" through social acceptance, money, or mental acuity.

With all of this grey area, it seems obvious that more people would be mentally and emotionally struggling than they did prior, despite having more physical challenges to overcome.

Recovery comes down to something very simple, which is restoring the feeling of one's safety.

However, the most important part of this restoration is

that you must reestablish a feeling of safety in the exact area of life that traumatized you.

Often, if someone is traumatized by a relationship they had when they were young, they will reinvest that energy into valuing being attractive or successful. To them, they believe that if they are "good enough," they can never be denied or rejected again. However, we all know this is not how this works. It actually makes us have unhealthy and destructive attachments to these things.

If we are traumatized by a relationship, we restore the feeling of safety by working on other healthy, safe relationships.

If we are traumatized by money, we restore the feeling of safety by doing what we must to ensure we have enough and by saving for an emergency expense.

If we are traumatized by job loss, we restore the feeling of safety by having a backup plan or a side gig in line in case it were to happen again.

If we are traumatized by being bullied, we restore the feeling of safety by finding new friends.

What most people try to do is overcompensate in an area of life that is not the real problem. For example, if they struggled in relationships, they hoard money to keep themselves feeling "safe." Of course, this is always futile, because the problem never gets solved.

Your trauma is not "in your head"; it is literally a changed state in your brain, and the only way you will help your body to return to its actual state is by recreating the feeling of safety that allows you to "turn off" survival mode and return to normal life.

RELEASING EMOTIONAL BACKLOG

Your emotional backlog is like your email inbox.

It might be a simple analogy, but it's an effective one. When you experience emotions, it's as though you're getting little messages from your body stacking up one at a time. If you don't ever open them, you end up 1,000+ notifications deep, totally overlooking crucial information and important insights that you need to move your life forward. At the same time, you can't sit around all day and respond to every message just as it comes up; you'd never get anything done.

It is a mistake to assume that emotions are optional experiences. They are not. But we are masters of avoiding our feelings, and we do it in so many ways. Often, we rely on substances that physically numb us, projections and judgments that place the attention on someone else's faults as opposed to our own, all kinds of other worldly pursuits, and on the most basic level, tensing our bodies up so efficiently that we are rendered incapable of feeling.

Psychologically, you probably know that this doesn't work for long. The backlog starts to jam eventually. You are forced to sit and be still and sleep and cry and feel it all.

I wish there were some poetic, mystical truth to share here, but there isn't. There is only your anatomy, the physiology of what's happening inside you when you feel.

Emotions are physical experiences. We flush our bodies of everything, and regularly so. We defecate, we sweat, we cry, we literally shed our entire skin once a month. Feelings are no different; they are experiences that must likewise be released.

When not felt, emotions become embodied. They become literally stuck in your body. This is because they have something called a motor component, which means that the minute they begin—before you can suppress or ignore them—they create a micro-muscular activation.

Our bodies respond instantaneously.

We often store pain and tension in the area of the body where an expression began but was never fully materialized.

This is because, neurologically speaking, the part of your brain that regulates emotions, the anterior cingulate, is next to the premotor area, which means that when a feeling is processed, it immediately begins to generate a physical, bodied response. The premotor area connects to the motor cortex and then spans back into the specific muscles that are going to express the emotion.

Which muscles express which emotion? Well, it depends.

We have a lot of language that clues us into where we have physical reactions to emotions. We often feel fear in our stomachs (think of a nervous stomach, or a "gut instinct") and heartache in our chests (that's where the whole "broken heart" thing comes from), stress and anxiety in our shoulders (think of the "weight of the world on your shoulders"), and relationship problems in the neck (think "they are a pain in the neck").

But it actually goes even deeper than this. Let's say that someone did something to you that crossed a boundary, and your instinct was to yell at them. However, because you understood it was not effective to literally scream, you held back. Though this may have been the right thing to do in the moment, your body may be storing residual tension in the neck or throat area. In other cases, people can experience psychosomatic effects of their emotions that are a bit more abstract, such as pain in their knees or feet when they are traumatized by "moving forward" in their lives, and so on.

The truth is that our bodies are speaking to us in voiceless symbols. If we can learn to interpret what they are saying, we can heal ourselves in an entirely new way.

So you know that emotions sometimes get stored in your body when they are not fully expressed. Be this as it is, how do we begin to flush ourselves from them?

There are a number of strategies that you can use to do this, and what matters is that it's effective for you. There is no one-size-fits-all, but there are a few options that tend to work well for most people, particularly when they are used in tandem.

STOP MEDITATING TO FEEL CALM; START MEDITATION TO JUST *FEEL*.

I know that this goes against everything you've ever heard about meditation. But it is actually the point of meditation. If you sit down for a 10-minute session and try to force yourself to be relaxed and light, you are effectively doing the exact same type of suppression that likely gave you the need to meditate in the first place.

Instead, the point of meditation is to sit idly as you experience all of those feelings come up: the rage, the fear, the sadness, the overwhelming mind chatter...and in spite of how alluring or triggering it may be, you learn to stay still and not respond to it. You learn to allow these thoughts and feelings to come up and then pass by virtue of you not reacting to them.

This takes practice.

USE BREATH SCANS TO FIND RESIDUAL TENSION IN THE BODY.

It usually doesn't take too much extra effort to figure out where in your body you are storing pain. You feel it. It's in your chest, your stomach, your shoulders, whatever is bothering you.

However, if you aren't sure, or if you want to zero in specifically on where that pain is, do something called a breath scan. In this, you will breathe in and out slowly, and without taking a break between breaths. When you do this, you will begin to notice that you might hit a "snag" or hiccup somewhere, that in the process of taking your breath, you will start to feel precisely where in your body you are storing tension.

Once you know, you can start to go into that feeling more, visualizing what it is, where it came from, and what it needs you to know. Often in this scenario, we are brought back to specific memories or past versions of ourselves that need assistance or guidance. Use a journal to write down what you experience and see, and remember that the body often speaks in metaphors, so don't necessarily take everything literally.

SWEAT, MOVE, CRY.

The last, the hardest, and the most important part of releasing your emotions is really the only thing you have to do...you have to feel them.

Sometimes, this means allowing yourself to feel like total shit. Sometimes, this means pushing yourself through a workout, yoga, stretching, walking, or confronting triggering thoughts and letting yourself cry out what's bothering you.

Remember that emotional health is not the experience of being perpetually calm and happy all of the time. It is the experience of allowing a range of emotions, both good and bad, and not getting too stuck on either one. Similarly, mental health and self-mastery is the ability to see and feel and experience a thought without responding to it. The response, or lack thereof, is where we regain our power and reclaim our lives.

You were not born to be perfect.

You were not born to be happy all of the time.

But if you can commit each day to doing the work of being fully human and feeling even when you are afraid, you can transcend in a way that is truly beautiful.

WHAT IT REALLY MEANS TO HEAL YOUR MIND

Healing your mind is not the same thing as healing your body. When you're physically wounded, you often go through a progressive, linear repair. You get better until one day you are nearly back to where you were before.

Healing your mind is completely different, because you aren't returning to what you were before. You are gutting yourself and becoming someone entirely new.

If that seems a little bit violent and harsh, it should. Healing is not a lovely ascension into comfort and wellness to be experienced once and forevermore. Healing yourself is the most uncomfortable, disruptive, important thing you will ever do.

Healing yourself is returning to your most natural state, which is hungry for personal freedom, irreverent to the suffocating opinions of others, creates without doubt, shows up without fear, and loves without stipulations and agreements and conditions. Who you truly are is at once the best version of yourself you might not have ever imagined and the most essential version of yourself that you have always been.

And getting to that place? It requires a lot.

Healing requires you to take an honest inventory of your grudges and aggressions and the wells of longing and fear you've been ignoring all this time. It requires you to take stock of precisely what is wrong with your life so you can work to make it right. It requires you to be completely honest about how you really feel, and then it requires you to actually feel it.

Healing requires you to feel the deep heartache lingering

in you instead of subconsciously re-creating the experience so you have an outlet to release it. Healing is no longer trying to sanitize your experience, to cleanse it until it is made perfect.

Healing requires you to go through the full expression of every emotion that you cut off and buried when you decided you were no longer comfortable with it. Healing requires you to face every ounce of darkness within you, because just beneath what appears to be an impermeable barrier is complete, radical, total freedom. When you are no longer scared to feel anything, when you no longer resist any one part of your life, something magical happens: You find peace.

Let's be clear: You are not going to suffer forever. This is not going to hurt for long. But to trick yourself into thinking that healing is getting progressively better until you have unraveled all of your past experiences and can return to the version of yourself you were before you got hurt...well, that is to miss the point entirely.

We are meant to go through these periods of what some refer to as positive disintegration. It is when we must adapt our self-concept to become someone who can handle, if not thrive, in the situation that we are in.

This is healthy. This is normal. This is how we are supposed to respond.

But we cower, because it will be uncomfortable. It will not immediately give us the virtues of what we are taught is a worthwhile life: comfort and ease and the illusion that everything is perfect on the surface.

Healing is not merely what makes us feel better the fastest. It is building the right life, slowly and over time. It is greeting ourselves at the reckoning, admitting where we've faltered. It is going back and resolving our mistakes, and going back within ourselves and resolving the anger and fear and small-mindedness that got us there in the first place.

Healing is refusing to tolerate the discomfort of change because you refuse to tolerate mediocrity for one second longer. The truth is that there is no way to escape discomfort; it finds us wherever we are. But we are either going to feel uneasy pushing past our self-imposed limits, breaking boundaries and becoming who we dream of being, or we're going to feel it as we sit and mull over fears we fabricated to justify why we refuse to stand up and begin.

Healing is going to be hard at first. It is going to mean looking at yourself honestly, maybe for the first time ever. It is going to mean stepping out of your comfort zone so you can leap toward the person you want to be. It is not what makes you more comfortable and idle. It is what conditions you to be more motivated by discomfort than you are scared of it, and inspired by your still moments more than you use them to forge the chains of worry.

Healing is going to change everything, but it has to start with you being willing to feel what you are afraid to feel.

Let's be clear about something: Becoming the best version of yourself is your natural inheritance. It is what you are born to do. Healing is simply releasing the sickness that is the limiting beliefs and fears that are holding you back from doing exactly that.

Healing is not about going back to exactly who you were before, because that person wasn't yet capable of seeing the storm before it hit, and that person didn't know how to shield themselves from it.

You aren't supposed to go back to being naive, less jaded, or more unaware. You aren't meant to return to your blissful mindlessness, a life in which you didn't know about the contrasts, the pain, all of the good and bad that life can throw at you.

What you get on the other side of healing is greater than that; you just haven't experienced it yet to know. What you get for going through something painful is that you become more resilient, more self-sufficient, more empowered.

You realize that nothing will save you, and so you must begin the work of saving yourself, which is the entire purpose of your life.

When you begin this work, you find your inner strength. You realize that you have power and influence and you can strategize and redirect your life. You realize that instead of what you can't control, your life can be built on what you do.

When you heal, you become stronger where you've been broken. You become grounded where you've been egotistical. You become responsible where you've been neglectful. You become more sensitive and able and conscious. You become more considerate, you are more empathetic, you are more mindful, more careful.

But what you don't need to be more of is afraid.

Fear is not going to protect you. Action is. Worrying is not going to protect you. Preparing is. Overthinking is not going to protect you. Understanding is.

When we hold onto fear and pain after something traumatic has passed, we do it as a sort of safety net. We falsely believe that if we constantly remind ourselves of all the terrible things that we didn't see coming, we can avoid them. Not only does this not work, but it also makes you less efficient at responding to them if they do.

Because most of the time, you're so busy worrying about monsters in the closet, you forget to address the actual things that will erode you over time: your health, your relationships, your long-term vision, your finances, your thoughts.

When you heal completely, you stop tolerating discomfort. When something is wrong, you recognize that it is wrong and take action to fix it because you've seen what happens when you don't.

When you heal completely, you are able to think ahead and rationally consider cause and effect. You recognize that your actions will generate results, and if you want to better control the outcomes of your life, you have to better adjust your habits.

When you heal completely, you realize that there is nothing more important than being able to enjoy where you are, right here and right now. Whatever obstructions are in the way of you being present and savoring your life are the challenges you have to face.

Because life is quick, and it's temporary. What you have now you could lose tomorrow, and gripping it so tightly, binding it up with resistance doesn't mean it's safer. It means that when the day comes that it passes—as does everything, as does everyone—you will realize you never really enjoyed it.

And healing? It's about getting to a place where you prioritize nothing over the quality of your one, short life.

MOVING FORWARD ISN'T ABOUT GETTING REVENGE

Your glow up might not be something others can see. It might not come across as a shift on the surface.

In a world of revenge bodies and comeback relationships, a world that tries to tell you that your ultimate transformation should be splayed out across your Instagram feed, we've lost what it really means to heal, to improve, to move on with our lives.

The real glow up isn't proving the people from your past wrong. It is finally feeling so content and hopeful about your future that you stop thinking about them entirely.

When you want to change your life so it looks different, and only that, you are still orbiting around the opinions of people who didn't love you and didn't have any intention to.

You can always tell the difference, too. People who have truly transformed are not concerned solely with how things appear. Their lives are now focused intently on how things *feel,* how they really are underneath it all.

A real glow up is authentic. It is lifting off all the cover-up bullshit and addressing the real problems. It is healing. It is changing, for good. It is, for the first time, prioritizing your heart over someone else's eyes.

Anyone can piece together an image that looks better. Anyone can edit and filter and lay picture after picture, side by side, to create a narrative, a story, a semblance of the whole. Anyone can buy their way into beauty, anyone can look nicer if they really try, anyone can convince you that they are doing better than they really are.

If they are so intent on trying to prove that, it is probably because they are still so empty inside.

What if you weren't worried about whether or not you look bigger or smaller or nicer or better than you did 10 years ago?

What if you were more concerned about whether or not you gain self-respect, real relationships, emotional freedom, mental clarity, a job you appreciate, work you respect, a kinder and more empathetic disposition?

What if your accomplishments were not something you could photograph or measure, nothing you could loosely try to communicate across some pixels and status updates? How are you feeling today? Better than you did yesterday? More whole, more confident?

The truth is that there is no before and after in life. We are always in a process of shedding and becoming. That snapshot moment you're waiting for, that instance in which someone dares to look you up again and sees, finally, that you are thriving...is a game for you, and you alone.

Nobody is looking at you the way you think they are. Nobody is thinking about you the way you wish they would. They are looking at themselves. They are thinking about themselves.

They are reading themselves.

This isn't sad; it's freeing. This should be the crux of your ultimate liberation.

The truth is that you have nobody to prove wrong but yourself. The people from your past probably didn't disapprove of you nearly as much as you feared they did.

This closure is for you. This growth is for you. This change is yours. This is you vs. you, you meeting you, you seeing you for the first time. This is about you becoming who you know you can be. This is about you finally living up to your potential.

But mostly, this is about you recognizing that you were not your best self before.

You didn't behave the way you wish you would have.

You didn't do what you should have.

You weren't what you hoped you'd be.

Whenever we want desperately to prove someone else

wrong, we are really trying to quell our own lingering disappointment that we didn't live up to our own expectations.

So remember this: The next time you're trying to craft a glow up story that is compelling to others, ask yourself why you are still waiting for their approval.

The answer, almost always, is that you still do not have your own.

CHAPTER 6

BUILDING A NEW FUTURE

NOW THAT YOU HAVE done the challenging work of beginning to release your past experiences, you must turn your attention toward building a new present and future. When we release, we are wiping the slate clean to create something better.

One of the most common pitfalls of people who try but do not succeed in releasing their past is that their focus remains on just that—the past. The work now is to envision who you want to be, connect with the most powerful version of yourself, design your life through your daily routine, and uncover your true purpose for being.

MEETING YOUR HIGHEST POTENTIAL FUTURE SELF

A popular tool in psychotherapy is something called inner child work[15], or the process of imagining and reconnecting with your younger self. In this process, you can offer yourself guidance, even going back to certain traumatizing events and readdressing them with the wisdom you have now.

But more often, the process of reconnecting with your inner child is to let them communicate with you. It is how you can rediscover your inherent desires, passions, fears, and feelings.

The process is akin to reverse engineering, which is when you identify the end goals for your life and then work backwards to see what you need to do each day, week, month, and year to get there. However, it works the opposite way as well. You can use a visualization technique to connect to your highest potential future self.

STEP 1: FACE THE FEAR FIRST

Sit down in a quiet place with a journal. Make sure you're doing it at a time when you feel relaxed and open to receive guidance. If you go into this with fear, you are going to get fear.

Next, close your eyes and begin a meditation session. Take a few moments to breathe deeply and center yourself. Imagine sitting down at a comfortable table in a well-lit room, somewhere that you are happy and feel at peace.

Then, invite your future self to come sit with you and talk. You can request that they are a certain age, but usually the age will just come to you when you see them.

Specifically ask for the highest possible version of yourself to sit down. If you see anything scary at first, know that it is your fear of what could happen manifesting in your mind, not the truth of what will happen.

Once you get past that, you can start receiving advice.

STEP 2: NOTICE HOW YOUR FUTURE SELF LOOKS

Aside from what you imagine this version of yourself telling you, pay attention to what they look like, how they behave, and what their facial expressions communicate.

The point of doing future self work is so that you can merge with this aspect of yourself. You want to clearly envision the most ideal version of yourself so that you know how your own life needs to grow, shift, and change.

See what they wear, how they feel, what they do each day. These will be the keys to your own becoming.

STEP 3: ASK FOR GUIDANCE

If you go into this process with a laundry list of scary, huge questions for your future self to answer, you're probably going to end up bound by panic rather than being open to receiving powerful guidance.

Instead, keep yourself open to whatever this person wants to share with you. The messages should be positive, uplifting, affirming, and helpful. Even if they communicate something to you such as, *you need to let go of this relationship*, it should be done in a way that is so calming and reaffirming that you are confident and at peace with it.

STEP 4: IMAGINE THEM HANDING YOU THE "KEYS" TO YOUR NEW LIFE

Another powerful exercise using your future self is to imagine yourself now sitting down with yourself 3, 5, or even 7 years ago. It has to be close enough that you can relate to this person but far enough that you've changed.

Imagine sitting down in a space you used to frequent or inhabit. What you're going to do now is hand them the pieces of your current life and all of the information they will need to go from who they are then to who you are now.

You can hand them your car keys, your email account for your job, your bank account, an outfit, or instructions on what to do in terms of career, relationships, or just day-to-day habits.

Or you can imagine your future self giving you aspects of your life now. Imagine them handing you the keys to the home you live in, or your wedding band, or anything else that is a part of your highest possible future life.

Remember, this process should make you feel calm, affirmed, and more self-assured, not the opposite. Fear is a hallucination, a trick of the mind and gut. Your future self can step in and remind you of all that is possible and empower you to live with certainty, clarity, and grace.

RELEASING YOUR PAST INTO THE QUANTUM FIELD

When something happens that scares you and then you do not ever get over that fear, you become traumatized.

Trauma is the experience of disconnecting with a fundamental source of safety. It happens most severely when our attachment to our primary caretakers is compromised. But there is truly an infinite number of ways the world can traumatize you, and to varying degrees.

There are lots of theories about what trauma is and where it comes from. Some believe that it is passed down physically through DNA.[16] Others argue that it is shared mentally and emotionally through learned patterns and observations. Most commonly, trauma is believed to be an interpersonal experience we have in which we were challenged and then lacked the skills and coping mechanisms to rise to it.

No matter where it came from, if you have some kind of lingering trauma, you will know, because you will feel it. You will feel it physically in your body. You will feel anxiety, tension, fear, terror, sadness, or guilt. It will be displaced. It will not have a clear, direct cause. You will overreact to certain things and even when a problem is solved, you will still panic. This is the mark of trauma.

TRAUMA IS NOT IN YOUR HEAD. IT IS IN YOUR BODY.

This is the first and most important thing you need to know in order to overcome it: Trauma is a legitimate, physical issue. You store those emotions, energies, and patterns at a cellular level.

Thankfully, we can use the ripples at the top of the water to trace back down to the problem at the bottom. You can begin to use your body to help you heal.

FIRST, IDENTIFY WHAT CAUSED THE TRAUMATIC EXPERIENCE.

You do this by feeling into yourself and noticing where you are tight or tense. Our bodies harden to protect us. When we have a broken leg, our fascia tightens like a natural cast so that we do not bend ourselves that way again. Similarly, when our hearts are broken, our emotions tighten so that we do not let ourselves feel again.

Of course, eventually, we have to walk. We have to love. We have to experience life again. We have to slowly soften the pieces of us that are trying to protect us so that we can move forward.

Healing trauma is not just a matter of psychoanalyzing it. It is a matter of literally working through it physically. The next time you feel yourself overreacting to some kind of stimulus, you will notice that your body is starting to tense up and create a fight-or-flight response. To heal this, you have to force yourself to take deep, soothing breaths until the part of your body that was once tense is relaxed again.

You will need to self-soothe in different ways: meditating, breathing, drinking enough water, getting enough sleep, using aromatherapy, sound therapy, or whatever else works for you.

You absolutely must work to take your brain and body physically out of panic/survival mode.

SECOND, REINSTATE A SENSE OF SAFETY.

You are traumatized because something scared you and you are convinced that it is still "out to get you." This is what happens when we don't face or overcome something difficult—we assume the threat lingers indefinitely.

The psychological aspect of trauma healing is that you have to literally restore the connection that was severed in the exact same way that it was broken.

If you are traumatized about relationships, you need to build healthy relationships. If you are traumatized about money, you need to get really good with money. If you are traumatized about traveling, you need to travel again.

We do not find the resolution in avoiding these things forever. In fact, just underneath the fear we often find that they are the things we really want more than anything else.

THIRD, STOP TAKING THOUGHTS AND FEELINGS AT FACE VALUE.

Last, to overcome trauma, you have to stop engaging in psychic thinking. You have to stop pretending you are able to predict what will happen, that you know other people's intentions, or that what you feel and think is absolute truth and reality.

This kind of thinking is what takes a triggering feeling and turns it into a defeating spiral. You take one scary thing and make it into a prediction for what the future will hold.

You are not an oracle. You do not know what's next, though you are always capable of choosing what you do now. Almost always, the thing you are most panicked about is a thing you do not know is happening for sure. It is usually an assumption, a projection, a fear turned into a terrifying potential reality.

You might think that trauma is something that other, more damaged people have, but that is not true. Everyone is traumatized in one way or another, but it is how we respond to it, how we ultimately grow and develop self-mastery from it, that determines the course of our lives.

BECOMING THE MOST POWERFUL VERSION OF YOURSELF

Are you being the most powerful version of yourself?

If you had to pause to think about it, the answer is probably no.

Everybody has different facets of their personality, and we act on them based on the context we're in. It's a social adaptation tool: You are not the same person with your friends as you are with your parents. Moving through these easily is a sign of high psychological function.

We are acquainted with the versions of ourselves that our current life requires. We know who we need to be at work, at home, or in love. But we are often unfamiliar with the person we need to be in order to move our lives forward.

In "inner child work," you visualize and address your younger selves, often down to a specific age, depending on which version of you was traumatized. You communicate with that inner child self, learn from them, protect them, or give them the guidance that they needed when they were young.

This proves to be profoundly healing for people, mostly because we do not evolve past our former selves; we simply grow upon them.

However, this practice can work the opposite way as well. You can also visualize and connect with your future self—the version of you that you are growing into, or the person you know you are meant to be.

WHAT WOULD MY MOST POWERFUL SELF DO TODAY?

The first step to becoming your most powerful self is to literally envision that person. Don't take yourself out of your current context, either. Begin to ask yourself: What would the most powerful version of me do right now? What would they do with this day? How would they respond to this challenge? How would they move forward? How would they think? What would they feel?

Your most powerful self needs to be the CEO of your life. It is the person making managerial decisions, governing everything else. This is the editor-in-chief, the matriarch or patriarch. You are working for your most powerful self.

Once you have a clearer image of what your most powerful self is like, you then need to evaluate what habits, traits, and behaviors are actively holding you back from fully embodying that person.

BE AWARE OF YOUR WEAKNESSES

Powerful people are not delusional. They do not believe they are perfect all the time at everything. This is not what makes them mentally strong. Instead, powerful people are very aware of their varying strengths and weaknesses.

In business, powerful people will often outsource the tasks at which they are less skilled. In life, powerful people know where their limits are and what their triggers might be. This allows them to move through their lives with more ease and to give themselves the time and space needed to work on their faults.

The ability to say to yourself: "I know I struggle a lot with this, so I'm going to take my time and work on it" is one of the most powerful things you can do.

BE WILLING TO BE DISLIKED

Powerful people are not the ones who are most universally liked.

They are also not the ones vying for others' approval, and that's the key.

To be a truly powerful person, you must be willing to be disliked. This is not to say that you behave in any way that's malicious, but it is to say that no matter what you do, others are going to judge you. Powerful people know this. There is no path in life that you can take that will be free of resistance from others, and so it is important that you not only become okay with being disliked, but you anticipate it and act anyway.

ACT ON PURPOSE

Powerful and purposeful are one in the same.

To be a truly powerful person, you need to have complete, unwavering conviction about what you want to create. To do this, you have to shift from a "live for the moment" to a "live for the legacy" mindset.

Your purpose is a dynamic, evolving thing. Most of the time, it is at the intersection of what you are interested in, what you are good at, and what the world needs. Having a clear vision of what you want to create and accomplish is essential to finding your inner power. You will not feel strongly about a dream that is not part of who you most essentially are.

DO YOUR INNER WORK

This is perhaps the most important and yet most commonly overlooked, because it is the least comfortable.

To do your inner work means to evaluate why something triggered you, why something is upsetting you, what your life is trying to show you, and the ways you could grow from these experiences. Truly powerful people absorb what has happened to them and sort of metabolize it. They use it as an opportunity to learn, to develop themselves. This type of inner mental and emotional work is non-negotiable if you want to be truly powerful.

Powerful people are not the most aggressive; aggression is usually a self-defense mechanism. Powerful people are the ones most unfazed by small disturbances and most willing to fully process and work through the big ones.

Of course, this is the foundational stuff. Next, you have to work on simplifying your life, talking less about your ambitions, and showing more of your accomplishments once they are completed. Gradually make health improvements. Assume that everyone, and everything, has something to teach you. Become comfortable with vulnerability, as vulnerability precedes almost every significant part of your life, and intentionally design your daily routine.

Through everything, you must be thinking as your most powerful self would. If you learn to see the world and your life through that lens, you can create a life that reflects the intentions of that side of you. It already exists; you just need to know how to tap into it.

LEARNING TO VALIDATE YOUR FEELINGS

If we want to be effective in therapy, in politics, in relationships, in teaching kids, in talking someone down from the edge, in keeping peace, making friends, fostering connection, and making progress, there's one technique we have to employ first.

It's a little secret, and it's one that requires very little effort. But it disarms people. It opens them, makes them receptive, willing to listen and adapt. It is healing, it is mind-altering, but most importantly, it is the first step to progress. It is emotional validation.

Validating someone's feelings doesn't mean you agree with them. It doesn't mean you concede that they are correct. It doesn't mean that those feelings are the healthiest; it doesn't mean they are informed by logic. Validating feelings does not mean you make them more true; it means you remind someone that it is human to feel things they don't always understand.

How often do we just need a partner to stop trying to strategize and just say, *that must really suck*?

How much of a weight is lifted off our shoulders when we think: *Yes, I really am stressed right now, and I deserve to be*?

How light do we feel when we see another person's story

splayed out across a screen, one that we can relate to, and understand, no matter how devastating it is?

How much better do we feel when we simply allow ourselves to be aggrieved and pissed-off and irrationally mad?

When we let ourselves have it—the feeling, that is—something incredible happens. We no longer have to take it out on other people, because we are no longer relying on their validation to get us through it.

We can be aggrieved and pissed and mad and do our own processing without hurting anyone else.

When people are crying out or acting out in their lives, they aren't just asking for help. They are most often just asking for someone to affirm that it is okay to feel the way that they do. And if they have to inflate and exaggerate circumstances for you to truly feel the weight and impact that they do? They'll do it. They'll do whatever it takes to get someone else to say: *I am so sorry for what you are going through.* This is not because they are incompetent or dumb. It is because in a world that does not teach us how to adequately process our own feelings, we must often rely solely on our maladaptive coping mechanisms.

When we cannot validate our own feelings, we go on a never-ending quest to try to force others to do it for us, but it never works. We never really get what we need.

This looks like needing attention, affirmation, compliments. But it also looks like being dramatic, negative, and focusing disproportionately on what's wrong in our lives. When someone is complaining about something simple—and they seem to be doing it more than the given situation would call for—they aren't trying to get your help about a small issue. They are trying to have their feelings validated.

This is also a common root of self-sabotaging behaviors. Sometimes, when we have deep wells of grief within us, we absolutely cannot allow ourselves to relax and enjoy our lives and relationships. We cannot just "have fun," because doing so feels like a betrayal. It feels offensive. We need to feel validated, but we don't even know why.

WHY IS THIS EFFECTIVE?

Think of your feelings like water running through ducts in your body. Your thoughts determine whether or not the ducts are clean. The cleanliness of the ducts determines the quality of the water.

If you suddenly have a feeling that you dislike and don't expect—a sudden rush of water, let's say—it's common to want to shut that valve off and not allow it to pass. However, stopping the flow of water does not make the water go away. Instead, it begins to intensely pressurize and create serious damage to the parts of your body that are no longer receiving flow. This begins to have a ripple effect on your entire life.

Sometimes, the water disperses itself gradually. Other times, it implodes and creates what we see on the surface as a complete emotional breakdown. When all of that water finally comes through and we grieve and cry and fall apart, we are going through a process of being reset. It is positive disintegration: We are gutted, but at the same time, feel better when it's over.

All that happened in that implosion was that your feelings became validated when you gave yourself permission to feel them—because you had no other choice. This is what we do in therapy. This is what we do when we vent. This is what happens when we experience a catharsis. A sad movie that we kind of enjoy being sad about allows us to feel sad in a world that otherwise does not.

But there's a healthier, easier way, which is learning how to process our feelings in real time.

"Validating your feelings" sounds like a big term, but it really means one thing: It's just letting yourself have them.

When you are healing past trauma, often a big component is allowing yourself to experience the full expression of an emotion. You have probably done this in the past. Think about the passing of a relative whom you loved but were not overly attached to. When you learned of their death, you were undoubtedly sad. But you didn't attend their funeral, cry for an hour, and then carry on with your life as though nothing happened.

Instead, you probably experienced a bout of sadness then, and then maybe the next day, and then maybe a week later. The waves of grief came and went in varying intensity. When you didn't resist them, you cried and felt sad, or maybe took a nap, a hot bath, or a day off from work.

And then, without much effort from you, the feeling passed, and you felt better.

Once we have and acknowledge an emotion, it will often go away on its own. If there is no course of action to take—if all we really need to do is accept it—then we just have to let ourselves be there.

The reason we don't do this more naturally is because obviously we can't burst into tears at our desks every time we feel bothered by something. Turning off the water valve is perfectly fine, as long as we can go home and let it out later. It is okay to control when and where we process, and in fact, it's better when we learn to do it in a more stable, safe space.

This can look like taking a few minutes to "junk journal" each day, spending time by ourselves where we can simply experience how we feel, without judgment, and without trying to change them. It can be as simple as allowing ourselves to cry before we fall asleep. We often think of that as a sign of weakness, when really, the ability to cry freely is a huge signal of mental and emotional strength. It's when we can't cry about what's truly broken in our lives that we have a big problem.

Validating the way someone else feels is an exercise in radial empathy. It is starting the conversation with: "It is okay to feel this way." Because when we point out how wrong someone is to feel the way they do, they shut down. And they shut down because they feel shame. They already know it's not right to feel the way they do. If you start the conversation by heightening someone's defenses or making them panic and suppress even harder, you make the situation worse.

But if you start with reminding them that anyone in their situation would probably feel similar to how they do right now, and that it is very possible that they can have strong, overwhelming emotions that don't necessarily mean their lives are completely ruined, and that it is okay to feel devastated when devastating things are before us, we lighten their load. We know this because when we stop resisting feeling sad and just let ourselves be sad, we realize that it will not last forever. We see that sometimes, the biggest problem isn't that we are devastated, but that in refusing to accept what is in front of us, we create so much more suffering than we would if we had just had a cry when we needed to have a really good cry.

Validating other people teaches us how to validate ourselves. And when we learn how to validate ourselves, we become stronger. We see that our emotions are no longer threats, but informants. They show us what we care about, what we want to savor, and what we want to protect. They remind us that life is fleeting, and challenging, and gorgeous. When we are willing to accept the darkness, it is only then that we find the light.

ADOPTING YOUR OWN PRINCIPLES

If you feel lost, or as though you don't know where you want your life to go next, or worse, fear that everything you have built could come crashing down, you don't need more inspiration. You don't need more positive thinking.

When you have money problems, you need money principles.

When you have relationship problems, you need relationship principles.

When you have work problems, you need work principles.

When you have life problems, you need life principles.

More money does not solve money problems. Different relationships do not solve relationship problems. New work does not solve work problems. Your future life will not solve your life problems.

This is because money does not make you good with money. Love does not make you love yourself. Relationships don't make you good at relationships. Work doesn't make you good at your job or capable of work/ life balance.

Problems don't inherently make you a stronger person unless you change and adapt. The variable here is you. The common denominator is whether or not you shift your foundational perspective on the world and how you behave within it.

Let's be very clear: Someone who makes $500K can be as seriously in debt and struggling as someone who makes $50K, and in fact, this happens more often than you would ever think. People who make less money are required to learn how to manage it better, and people who make more think they can eschew principles because of the quantity they are attaining.

You can screw up your dream relationship just as quickly as you can a hook up, because the way you relate to others is an issue with you, not something that shifts depending on whether or not you meet the most perfect person who never triggers or annoys you and relates to you with unconditional positive regard.

You can be just as unhappy in your ideal job, with your perfect hours, at your most desired pay rate, if you don't know how to ration your time, relate to others in your workplace, or move your career forward. People who are "living their dreams" and "following their passion" can be just as unhappy as people who are not.

If you don't have principles, your life is not going to get better. Problems are only going to follow you and get bigger as your life does.

The good things that happen to us in life are like a magnifier. They show us where we still need to grow. True love shows us to ourselves. Money shows us to ourselves. Dream jobs show us to ourselves. The good, the bad, the desperately-needs-to-change-right-now.

If you don't have principles now, you won't have them later. If you don't have the money principle of living beneath your means, you won't be able to do it when you have more money. If you don't have the relationship principle of not relying on others for your sense of self, it won't magically resolve itself when you meet the "right person"; you will only sabotage that relationship, too.

WHAT IS A PRINCIPLE?

A principle is a fundamental truth that you can use to build the foundation of your life. A principle is not an opinion or a belief. A principle is a matter of cause and effect.

Principles can be personal guidelines.

Some examples of money principles are the following: Keep overhead costs low, get out and stay out of debt, live beneath your means, or save for a rainy day.

Many financial experts advocate prioritizing debt repayment as the beginning of financial health. This is because one day of accrued interest probably won't impact you that much. But 20 years will, to the tune of tens of thousands of dollars, if not more.

In the same way, one day of gained interest in investments won't make a big difference. But 20 years will, to an even more significant margin.

The point of having principles is that it shifts you from short-term survival to long-term thriving.

Most things in our lives are governed by principles. Stephen Covey explains this well: Principles are a natural law like gravity. It's different than a value. Values are subjective; principles are objective.[17] "We control our actions, but the consequences that flow from those actions are controlled by principles," he says.

This means that if we are committed to the principle of eating good food each day, we will inevitably reap the benefit of better or improved health. If we write a sentence each day for many, many years, we will inevitably write a larger piece of work. If we commit to paying off a portion of our debts each month, we will inevitably clear our balance. If we invest consistently and wisely, we will eventually see a return.

Our lives are governed by principles, as Benjamin Hardy explains: "Most people cram for tests while in college. But can you cram if you're a farmer? Can you forget to plant in the spring, slack-off all summer, and then work hard during the fall? Of course not. A farm is a natural system governed by principles."[18]

So are you.

"The law of the harvest is always in effect. What you plant, you must harvest. Furthermore, what you plant consistently over time eventually yields a compounded or exponential harvest. You often don't experience the consequences of your actions immediately, which can be deceiving. If you smoked one cigarette, you probably wouldn't get cancer. If you spent $10 on coffee just one day, it probably wouldn't affect your financial life. However, over time, these habits have drastic outcomes. It turns out that $10 daily over 50 years at 5% compounding interest becomes $816,000."[19]

When you make an investment, you don't expect to see a return that day. In the same way, you can go to sleep feeling accomplished knowing that you chipped away at your future just by adhering to your principles.

Little things, done repeatedly and over time, become the big things.

WHY IS INSPIRATION INEFFECTIVE HERE?

Inspiration can be misleading. Big dreams not backed by strategic plans are big flops waiting to happen.

Inspiration means you take a feeling and elaborate on it. You allow your mind to wander; you piece together pretty pictures and create an image of how you'd like your life to feel.

Principles are boring. They aren't inspiring. They are the laws of nature.

Principles are not immediately gratifying.

They do not make us feel better right away.

That's why we often reach for inspiration but find it to be ineffective. This is because we get our minds and hearts set on a vague idea of what we think we want without ever really evaluating whether or not we want to engage in the daily work and effort it would take to get there.

When we don't pair inspiration with the principles it takes to achieve those dreams, we become more lost and disappointed than ever before.

HOW DO I START DEVELOPING MY OWN PRINCIPLES?

Nobody is born with excellent principles; they are something that you learn.

However, there are many different principles in life, and some may contradict one another. That's why it's important to adopt your own, ones that fit your goals and your life.

BEGIN WITH THIS:

- What do you value? What do you genuinely care about?

- What feelings do you want to experience in your life?
- What makes you uneasy or gives you anxiety?

THE ANSWERS COULD BE SOMETHING LIKE THIS:

I value relationships, and so by principle, I am going to prioritize them when given the opportunity. Alternatively, by principle, I value honest and positive relationships, so I'm not going to be in dating limbo anymore; unless someone commits within a reasonable amount of time, I will regard their hesitation as a "no."

Perhaps you value financial freedom, and so by principle, you are going to put your extra cash toward repaying debt or building savings or investments. Perhaps you value travel and freedom, and so by principle, you are going to start working for yourself and always prioritize being able to work remotely or make your own schedule.

When you are clear on what your principles are, you can build your life from a genuine, healthy place. You can start working toward goals that support what you do and do not want to experience, that will make you the calmest and happiest version of yourself.

A good life is built from the inside out and is based on a foundation of self-conduct and prioritization. It's not as dreamy as a vision board, but it's a lot more effective.

FINDING YOUR TRUE PURPOSE

When you live in a world that is constantly telling you to follow your heart, trust your gut, quit your day job, and do what you love, it can be disheartening when you don't know where to start. When you start thinking that you don't know what to do with your life, what you really mean is that you don't yet know who you are.

Finding your purpose is not necessarily about realizing that you are destined to live in a monastery or devote your life to a singular vocation or goal. Your purpose is not one job, it is not one relationship, it is not even one career field. Your purpose is, first and foremost, just to be here. Your existence has shifted the world in a way that it is invisible to you. Without you, absolutely nothing would exist just as it is right now. This is important to understand, because if you start believing that your whole purpose in being alive is just a specific job or role you take on at home, what happens when you quit or retire, or when the kids grow up and you're no longer a parent?

You'll sink because you will falsely think that was your only reason for being.

Your purpose today may have been to offer someone a smile when they were at their lowest. Your purpose this decade may be the job you're in. When you realize that you are always impacting the world around you, you start to realize something: The most important thing you can do to live meaningfully is to work on yourself. To consciously become the happiest, kindest, and most gracious version of yourself.

Knowing your purpose also doesn't necessarily mean your life will henceforth be easy or that you'll always know what to do. In fact, when you are genuinely on your own path, the future won't be clear, because if it is, you're actually following someone else's blueprint.

With all of that said, when most people wonder about their purpose, they are often referring to their life's work and their jobs. Your career is not nothing. It is how you will spend the majority of your day, every day, for the better part of your life. That's why figuring out how you can best serve the world through that makes the long days and difficult moments bearable.

Your life purpose is the point at which your skills, interests, and the market intersect.

You are the blueprint of your future. Everything that you are, everything that you have experienced, everything that you're good at, every circumstance you have found yourself in, everything that you're passionate about is not random; it's a reflection of who you are and a sign about what you are here to do.

However, it's not as easy as it sounds to become self-aware. You may still be thinking that you're not sure what you're good at, or that you're even more passionate about one thing over another. That's okay because your purpose does not require you to be the best at something.

It is not the thing at which you, and only you, can succeed more so than anyone else. It is the things that naturally call you, that effortlessly flow out of you, and that evoke specific emotions from you. You are here to work those out. You are here to transform them. Your ultimate purpose is to become the ideal version of yourself. Everything else flows from there.

FIGURING OUT WHAT YOU WANT TO DO WITH YOUR LIFE

Here are some questions you should ask yourself if you want to know what your purpose really is:

WHAT, AND WHO, IS WORTH SUFFERING FOR?

Even doing what you love for a living doesn't mean every day will be easy. Everything comes with its own set of challenges, so the question is really: What are you willing to work for? What are you willing to be uncomfortable for?

CLOSE YOUR EYES AND IMAGINE THE BEST VERSION OF YOURSELF. WHAT IS THAT PERSON LIKE?

The best possible version of yourself—the most loving, kind, productive, and self-aware version—is who you really are. Everything else is the byproduct of coping mechanisms you've developed and picked up from other people.

IF SOCIAL MEDIA DIDN'T EXIST, WHAT WOULD YOU DO WITH YOUR LIFE?

If you knew that you wouldn't be able to show off, impress, or even share what it was you chose to do with your life, how would it change your ambitions? This differentiates what you are doing because you want to do it from what you are doing for the sake of how it looks to other people.

WHAT COMES MOST NATURALLY TO YOU?

What you are most naturally good at is the path you should follow first, because it's the path on which you will most effortlessly thrive.

WHAT WOULD YOUR IDEAL DAILY ROUTINE LOOK LIKE?

Forget about the elevator speech. Forget about having a fancy title or impressing people on LinkedIn. Think about what you want to do day-in and day-out. A lot of people get into jobs they think will make them happy but realize they only liked the idea of them and not the day-to-day reality.

WHAT DO YOU WANT YOUR LEGACY TO BE?

Instead of worrying about the virtues on your résumé,

focus on the virtues of your eulogy. Who do you want to be remembered as? What do you want to be known for?

Though it's lovely to reflect on all of the virtues and talents of your life, here is an even more important part of finding your purpose: It is often found through pain. Most people come into awareness of their purpose not because they are effortlessly clear on what their talents are and how they can best utilize them, but because at some point, they find themselves lost, depleted, exhausted, and with their backs against the wall.

In experiencing hardship and challenge, we begin to realize what really matters to us. It sparks a flame that, when kindled through action and commitment, becomes a transformative fire.

If you listen to the stories of many of the most successful people in the world, they often begin with unimaginable hardship. In the face of the most unlikely situations, these people are forced into action. Comfort and complacency is not an option. They realize they must become the heroes of their own lives and the creators of their own futures.

At the end of your life, your purpose will be defined not by how you struggled, what circumstances you were in, or what you were supposed to do, but how you responded in the face of adversity, who you were to the people in your life, and what you did each day that slowly, in its own unique way, changed the course of humanity.

CHAPTER 7

FROM SELF-SABOTAGE TO SELF-MASTERY

MOVING FROM SELF-SABOTAGE to self-mastery sounds like an extraordinary transformation, when in reality it is the natural course of coming to understand that you were responsible for holding your life back, and so you are also capable of moving it forward.

CONTROLLING YOUR EMOTIONS VS. SUPPRESSING THEM

The Buddhists believe that controlling the mind is the path to enlightenment.[20] Enlightenment, by which they mean, spontaneous and true happiness.

The idea is simple in theory and complex in practice: By both exploring our understanding of the mind and training it to behave in a certain way, we sort of purify ourselves to experience the essential nature of what we are, which is, as they believe, joy.

If you've ever sat in a meditation class, you'll know that the first principle of mind control is the opposite of what you'd think: It's about letting go.

To truly master the mind, the Buddhists practice non-attachment, in which they sit placidly, breathe steadily, and allow thoughts to rise up, cohere, and then pass.

Their approach is that controlling the mind is actually a matter of surrendering to the mind, allowing it to behave as it pleases while regulating their reaction to it.

HOW DO YOU KNOW IF YOU'RE SUPPRESSING YOUR EMOTIONS OR CONTROLLING THEM?

Emotional suppression is a regulation strategy that people use when they do not have adequate coping mechanisms for their feelings.

The pattern is often this: The person denies or ignores their true reaction to a situation or experience, believes it will simply go away if they continue to disregard it, finds that their day-to-day lives are disrupted by a sense of unease, and one day, it all comes to a breaking point and they have an emotional outburst that they cannot control.

Therapy generally aims to help patients no longer suppress how they feel. Instead, they are encouraged to recognize those emotions but choose how they respond to them.

In the healing process, suppressing and controlling can seem like a fine line.

When someone cuts you off in traffic and you choose not to yell out your window, are you suppressing how you feel or controlling it? If your partner says yet another idiotic thing and you choose not to respond to it, are you suppressing how you feel or controlling it? If your coworker aggravates you consistently about a project and you choose not to say anything, are you suppressing how you feel or controlling it?

SUPPRESSING IS UNCONSCIOUS; CONTROLLING IS CONSCIOUS.

Suppressed emotions function similarly to unconscious biases. One such type of bias is confirmation bias, wherein your brain sorts through stimuli to bring your attention to facts or experiences that support what you already believe. Though you're not aware of the bias, it's still affecting you.

On the other hand, controlling your emotions involves becoming more conscious of how you feel. You are aware that you are angry, sad, or aggrieved, but you are choosing what you do about it. It is not really that you are controlling your emotions, but your behavior.

When you are suppressing your emotions, you don't know how you feel and your behavior seems out of control.

When you're controlling your emotions, you do know how you feel, and your behavior seems within your control.

The answer is that when you're in traffic, or in an argument, or dealing with a difficult coworker, you should be aware of how you feel but still in control of how you respond. Emotions are temporary, but behaviors are permanent. You are always responsible for how you choose to act.

We often think that the measure of physical strength is how much weight we can bear, how long we can run, or how pronounced our muscles are. In reality, physical strength is a measure of how efficiently the body runs itself, how capable it is of effectively performing day-to-day tasks and occasional challenges when they arise.

Mental health is the exact same way. It is not a measure of how happy we seem, how perfect things are, or how unconditionally "positive" we can be, but that we are able to move through day-to-day life and the occasional challenge with enough fluidity and reason that we aren't stifled or held back by ourselves.

Amy Morin very famously disclosed some of the things that mentally strong people don't do. Identifying their habits and behaviors is essential, but what if you just aren't there yet? If you want to become a mentally strong person, this is where you begin.

LEARNING TO TRUST YOURSELF AGAIN

Inner peace is the state of being connected to the deep internal knowing that everything is okay and always will be. The concept of finding one's "inner peace" has been part of spiritual and metaphysical practices for centuries and has just recently become more mainstream with the development of popular psychology.

Albert Camus once said: "In the midst of winter, I found there was, within me, an invincible summer."

That sums up the entirety of what inner peace really is: the understanding that no matter what is happening around you, there is a place of total knowing and calmness within you. Not only are you capable of returning to that place when you need to, but it's possible to *live your entire life* from there. The challenge is learning how to connect with it in the first place and rewire how you respond to your mind, which is always jumping from one worst-case scenario to the next.

You know when people reference knowing something "deep down?" They say things like: "I'm worried, but deep down, I know it's going to be okay." Or, "I'm angry at him, but deep down, I know he loves me." What do you think they are referencing? Where is deep down? They're talking about the place within them that has an infinite wisdom, a better understanding, and a more insightful perspective of what's going on. It isn't shaken by the stressors or fears that the mind wants to offer.

So much of the process of finding inner peace is being able to get to that "deep down" place where you know and feel that ultimately everything will be okay.

There's another metaphor in meditation in which calmness is compared to steadying a lake or a large body of water. Your thoughts and actions are like stones in the water: They create a ripple effect. The point of meditation is to make yourself quiet enough so that the water comes back to its natural stillness. You don't have to *force* the water to be still. It does it on its own when you stop interrupting it.

The same goes for finding inner peace. It's not so much something you have to create as it is something you have to return to.

CREATING ALIGNED GOALS

One of the most important parts of discovering your inner peace is that you trade in your desire for "happiness."

Unfortunately, happiness is fickle. It can lead you to being attached to certain achievements, belongings, or specific circumstances. It can lead you to become dependent on other people's opinions or life unfolding in a particular way. When your goal is happiness, you will always find just behind it a lingering sense of unhappiness—that's how balance and duality works. Inner peace, however?

That's the state in between the scales. When it's your goal, there's no way to lose.

This is difficult for most people, and often, people will continue to create stress, problems, and drama for themselves because their egos are still very much attached to thinking they need something external to make them feel good. This is the quintessential sign of someone who has not yet found their inner peace: They are searching, often frantically, for a sense of satisfaction, belonging, or worthiness outside of themselves.

So really, it's not that happiness isn't a virtuous thing to which you should aspire, or that happiness isn't something you're ever allowed to feel. The reality is that inner peace is the true happiness, and everything else is just a false means of trying to convince yourself that you are "okay."

Think about it this way: What do you typically imagine will bring you happiness? Money, a relationship, a promotion? What happens when you achieve those things? Consistently, throughout all of humankind, the answer is the same: You return to your baseline. This is because this kind of happiness is not real. It is only being completely at peace with whenever you are in any given day that you will find a genuine sense of wonder, presence, and joy.

WHAT DRIVES US AWAY FROM INNER PEACE IN THE FIRST PLACE?

With all this talk of how we have to "come back" to our place of inner peace, it brings up the question of why we ever got disconnected from it in the first place. This is important because understanding why we lose it is fundamental to finding it again.

When we grow up, we adapt to our environments. We adopt the beliefs and ideas of those around us. We alter our personalities so that we become safer; we believe the world can't hurt us. When we are children, we are more vulnerable than ever, and it's during this time that we pick up what can easily become lifelong coping mechanisms.

If we are not instructed from a young age to connect with our inner sense of peace, we will instinctively begin to trust the voice in our head. This is where we really get lost, because the thoughts that we have on any given day are largely the product of what the Buddhists would call the "monkey mind," or as a neurologist could explain it, the process of different receptors firing off and making associations with things that may or may not have anything to do with reality.

When we begin to trust our thoughts, we let them inform our feelings. This becomes a cycle and ultimately traps most people who aren't aware that it's happening. They have a weird or scary thought, have a subsequent strong feeling, and the combination of the two makes the situation feel real when it's actually a misunderstanding of your neurological process.

Of course, that doesn't mean that our thoughts are useless. It just means that they are not always reflective of reality and should be used as more of suggestions than anything else.

WHY CAN'T PEOPLE FIND THEIR INNER PEACE EASILY?

The answer is that they can; most people just aren't instructed on how to. But beyond that, most people are actually too scared to go into their own feeling states, because their inner child is too traumatized.

Everyone has an "inner child"; it is the part of you that is most innocent and pure, and it never goes away.[21] Over time, it is your responsibility for you to learn how to parent this inner child, who will honestly be the one to push you away from your inner peace. They will be the one to throw a tantrum and tell you that everything is falling apart and that you're going to die and that you should just give up.

In the same way that you wouldn't let a child run your waking life now, you can't always believe what your inner child is afraid of. You can, however, learn to work with them, heal them, and make them feel safe...in the way any good parent would.

Stephen Diamond explains it like this: "To begin with, the inner child is real. Not literally. Nor physically. But figuratively, metaphorically real. It is, like complexes in general, a psychological or phenomenological reality, and an extraordinarily powerful one at that." He argues that mental disorders and destructive behavior patterns are usually more or less related to unconscious parts of ourselves and were most often adopted in early life.

FINDING YOUR OWN PEACE

Finding inner peace isn't always so much about just sitting in the lotus position until wisdom becomes you; it's about making the uncomfortable decision to stay with your discomfort and to choose differently.

As Gail Brenner explains: "The inner war is perpetuated by resistance—that is, not wanting to feel the way we feel, not wanting people to do what they are doing, not wanting events to occur as they are occurring. Resistance wants to rewrite our personal histories and ensure that our plans materialize." She argues that inner peace is the only kind that exists because nothing else is in our control.[22]

Another really amazing way to find your inner peace is to constantly remind yourself that your worries are a fabrication of your mind's need to identify potential threats for survival, and true happiness is being here in the moment. If that's hard to believe, make a list of the following:

- Everything you have intensely worried about in your life. Go back as many years as you can, and be as detailed as you can.

- Every difficult situation you swore you would never get through or never get over.

- Every time you have genuinely felt happy and at peace.

Guaranteed, your responses to the first will bring a smile to your face in that they will remind you that you have worried constantly in your life, and yet they were mostly unfounded.

Your response to the second will also be relieving, because it will show you just how much pain you thought was insurmountable in your life and how, in retrospect, you don't really ever think about those things anymore.

Finally, your answers to the last question will remind you that your happiness has never come from things being perfect on the outside, but from you being present and open and connected to yourself and to the moment.

DETACHING FROM WORRYING

In the same way that it's easy to become addicted to substances or behaviors that allow us to avoid the present moment, worrying is chief among the coping mechanisms people use to distract themselves from what really matters.

Over time, you convince yourself that worrying equals being safe. You think that by running worst-case scenarios through your head again and again, you will be better prepared for them. This is completely false. Not only are you draining your energy imagining situations that are very often completely manufactured, but when you are already hypersensitive to any one of these fears or ideas, you will actually create those circumstances simply out of your avoidance or over-responsiveness to them.

You have to remember that among all the things to know about the "monkey mind," your head wants to constantly seek out situations and experiences that will affirm itself. If you believe something will be good, it will be. It might not look exactly how you imagined, but the outcome will be exactly what you expect.

Finding your inner peace is just connecting to your deepest wisdom. It's not something you have to create, justify, imagine, or reach for. It's always within you, it's always an option, and it's constantly a choice. You just have to make it.

REMEMBERING THAT YOUR FEELINGS ARE NOT ALWAYS FACTS

The most challenging part of all of this is arriving at a place where you can discern between which feelings are instinctive and informative and which are rooted in fear and ego.

In a world that constantly tells you that your gut knows everything and that your feelings are real, and that if you reach in deep enough, you'll uncover a well of wisdom that can guide you... it can be really easy to assume that every feeling and idea we have is not only real but is somehow forecasting what's going to happen in the future.

Your feelings aren't predictions. They are not fortune-telling mechanisms. They are only reflecting back to you what your current state of mind is. It's like having a nightmare: The monsters aren't real, but they could be metaphors for something you're worried about in your waking life.

What holds so many people back from finding their inner peace is the fact that they can't tell the difference between which is correct: their fear or their peaceful feeling.

Remember this: The feeling of peace is the one telling you the truth.

Your feelings aren't here to tell you what's going to happen. They're only here to inform you of where you are energetically and mentally and how you should respond to what happens around you. Fear is trying to scare you into staying small and keeping safe. It is a mortal, limited thing. The feeling of peace is trying to remind you that everything will be okay because it always is...and always will be, no matter what.

BECOMING MENTALLY STRONG

No matter who you are or what your purpose is in life, mental strength is going to be a key component in ensuring that you actualize all of the potential latent within you.

Mental strength is not a fixed trait. It's not something we inherently have or don't. Ironically, it's not necessarily easier to have if you aren't faced with many challenges in life. In fact, it is often people who are in the most difficult circumstances that are forced to develop the highest degrees of mental strength.

Being mentally strong is a process, and it is a practice.

This is where you can begin.

GET A PLAN, BECAUSE PLANS FIX PROBLEMS

Mentally strong people are planners.

They think ahead. They prepare. They do what's best for the long-term outcome.

You might think that this disconnects them from the moment, but the opposite is true. Worrying disconnects you from the moment. Overthinking disconnects you from the moment. When you are consistently sidelined from your own anxiety, it's because you don't have a plan regarding the thing that's making you scared.

Think about something you aren't scared of. Do you know why you aren't scared of it? Because you have a plan for what you'd do if it were to happen. So you're able to let go and be present.

Whether it's becoming financially healthy, improving your relationships, going to therapy, getting a new job, or pursuing a new career path or dream: If you don't have a plan, you're going to keep having a problem.

HUMBLE YOURSELF, BECAUSE IT'S NOT ALL ABOUT YOU

It seems like everyone is thinking about you, judging you, evaluating you, and determining your status in life. They aren't.

Social media has likened us all to mini-celebrities in our own circles: We become convinced that everyone around us is disproportionately concerned with the minutiae of our lives.

In a number of decades, you will be gone. Your home will be sold to a new family. Your job will be taken by someone else. Your kids will be adults. Your work will be done. This isn't supposed to depress you; it is supposed to liberate you.

Nobody is thinking about you in the way that you think they are thinking about you. They are mostly thinking of themselves. When you feel self-conscious for going grocery shopping in your sweatpants, please know that nobody cares and nobody is looking. When you feel anxious about your accomplishments or lack thereof, please know that for the most part, nobody cares and nobody is looking. This is true of absolutely everything in life.

Nobody is evaluating you the way you are evaluating you. They mostly take you at face value. Stop thinking that you're the sun that everyone revolves around. This world is not all about you. Your life isn't even all about you. The more you can put aside your spotlight complex, the more you're going to be able to relax.

ASK FOR HELP, BECAUSE YOU'RE NOT SUPPOSED TO KNOW EVERYTHING

We live in a specialized society.

People go to school; they apprentice and train to become very skilled at one task. They then market and sell this task in exchange for purchasing other people's expertise.

You are not supposed to know everything.

You are not supposed to be a financial expert; that's why you can hire one to do your taxes or advise your investing.

You are not supposed to be a master chef; that's why you can buy a cookbook or ask your mother for help. You are not supposed to be a world-class trainer; that's why you can book an appointment with one and learn. You are not supposed to understand the complexities of mental health and neuropsychology; that's why you can visit with a psychotherapist and learn how to get better.

You are not supposed to know everything. You're not supposed to be good at everything. This is why you have people whom you can hire or learn from. Cut yourself some slack, and focus on what you are proficient in. Outsource everything else.

KNOW WHAT YOU DON'T KNOW, AND STOP FALSE DICHOTOMOUS THINKING

The main reason that people sustain anxiety is due to long-term thinking in either/ors, otherwise known as false dichotomies.

This is a cognitive distortion in which you eschew an entire field of possibilities in favor of one or two polarized outcomes, neither of which are likely or reasonable.

If I lose my job, I am a failure. False.

If this relationship ends, I'll never find love again. False.

If this scary thing happens, I won't be able to go on. False.

Anxiety is caused by logic lapses, where there's a breach in your reasoning skills. You jump from one event to an unlikely conclusion, and because it makes you feel something strongly, you assume it to be true. Ultimately, you start thinking in dichotomies, which are not only ineffective, but also spook you so much that you are rendered incapable of actually handling your life.

STOP TRYING TO BE PSYCHIC, BECAUSE THIS IS A COGNITIVE DISTORTION

Given that our most fundamental human fear is of the unknown, it makes sense that we go through mental gymnastics to try to predict certain outcomes in our lives.

However, psychic thinking, or the idea that your feelings are premonitions, that you can "just know" what the future will hold, or that your fate is somewhere set in stone for you, makes you mentally weak. It places you in the passenger's seat when you need to be behind the wheel.

When you are engaging in psychic thinking, you're extrapolating. You're taking a single feeling or experience and making a long-term prediction about your life. It is not only false; it often becomes a self-fulfilling prophecy.

Stop trying to predict what you can't know, and start putting your energy toward building what you can. You and your life will be better for it.

TAKE RESPONSIBILITY FOR YOUR OUTCOMES—YES, ALL OF THEM

In the grand scheme of your life, the outcomes that really matter are the ones that are almost completely within your control. It's easier and less scary to pretend as though you are simply a cog in the wheel, but you're not.

If you actually put your energy toward learning to be productive, taking care of your health and wellness, improving your relationships and self-awareness, you'd have a radically different life experience. Every single one of those things is within your ability to change or at least influence greatly.

There are some things in life that are outside of your control. If you focus on them, you will miss something really important: the majority of your life is the direct result of your actions, behaviors, and choices.

LEARN HOW TO FEEL BETTER BY PROCESSING COMPLEX EMOTIONS

You are not supposed to feel happy all of the time. Trying to feel happy all of the time is not the solution; it's the problem.

Instead of the ability to sustain positivity at all times, mental strength requires that you develop the ability to process complex emotions such as grief, rage, sadness, anxiety, or fear.

When you do not know how to allow these feelings to pass through you, how to make sense of them, learn from them, or simply just allow them, you get stuck on them. You bury them, and then everything around you becomes a trigger that threatens to unleash the floodgates.

You might think it's about keeping a stiff upper lip, but it's not. It's about crying when life is sad, being angry in the face of injustice, and being determined to create a solution when a problem arises. That responsiveness, instead of reactiveness, defines mental strength.

FORGET WHAT HAPPENED AND FOCUS ON HOW YOU WILL MAKE IT RIGHT

Reflect on what went wrong, learn from what went wrong, and figure out how you're either going to make up for it or change the outcome in the future.

Then let it go.

The only time you're going to really hold onto the past is when you haven't fully learned from the past. When you have, you can apply those lessons to the present moment and create what you wanted to experience then.

Focusing on what happened disproportionately to what's happening now, or what you want to happen in the future, is what keeps you completely stuck. If you feel as though you truly failed yourself in some profound way, it becomes even more crucial that you move on and create the experience you desire now.

Your life is not over. You did not fail indefinitely, but you will if you never let go and try again.

TALK IT OUT, BECAUSE THINGS ARE OFTEN MORE COMPLICATED IN YOUR HEAD

If you feel really tangled up in your thoughts, feelings, and fears, talk to someone. Perhaps a mental-health professional or a trusted friend. If nobody is around, talk to yourself. Talk out your ideas as though you were speaking to someone else in front of you.

Sometimes, we need an objective third party to help us sort through complicated parts of life. Keeping it all buried in your head and heart often makes it worse. Letting it out into the open tends to simplify the problem, release the emotion, and help you move on.

TAKE YOUR TIME, BECAUSE YOU DON'T NEED TO FIGURE EVERYTHING OUT RIGHT NOW

Growth usually isn't a sweeping thing. It happens incrementally. It occurs in tiny bursts and small steps. This is because when we are growing, we are actually expanding and restructuring our comfort zones. We are readjusting to a new way of life, and if we shock our systems with too much change too fast, we often revert back to what we knew.

The most effective and healthy way to change your life is slowly. If you need instant gratification, make the goal the tiny step you take each day. Over time, momentum will build, and you'll realize that you're miles from where you started.

TAKE TRIGGERS AS SIGNALS, BECAUSE YOUR WOUNDS NEED YOUR ATTENTION

Triggers are not random; they are showing you where you are either most wounded or primed for growth.

If we can see these triggers as signals that are trying to help us put our attention toward some part of our lives that needs healing, health, and progress, we can begin to see them as helpful instead of hurtful.

You cannot ignore your problems. You cannot disregard your wounds. These are issues that you will need to unpack, process, learn from, and adapt your behavior accordingly. This won't only make you mentally stronger; it will also give you a better quality of life overall.

HONOR YOUR DISCOMFORT, BECAUSE IT'S TRYING TO TELL YOU SOMETHING

The greatest gift that life will hand you is discomfort.

Discomfort is not trying to punish you! It is just trying to show you where you are capable of more, deserving of better, able to change, or meant for greater than you have right now. In almost every case, it is simply informing you that there is more out there for you, and it is pushing you to go pursue it.

Instead of trying to pacify this discomfort, mental strength requires that you listen, learn, and begin to change your course.

If you can begin to see your life as a feedback mechanism that is reflecting who you are with the ultimate goal to help you live better and more fully, all of a sudden you realize that it was never the world standing in your way, but your own mind.

HOW TO TRULY ENJOY YOUR LIFE

If you were to ask, many people would undoubtedly agree that they believe the purpose of life is to enjoy it. However, so many people struggle to be present and actually experience their lives as they are. The culprits are varied and can include everything from unrealistic expectations to trying too hard to feel good. (It is, after all, something you have to allow.)

When you're struggling, the most insulting and difficult thing that someone can tell you is to "just relax" or "just enjoy yourself." When you're in survival mode, the last thing you can possibly think about is just sitting back and rolling with the punches. This is the most important part of learning how to enjoy your life again: When you're in a place of trauma and pain, you can't try to force yourself to be happy. First, you have to step back into neutral.

When you're struggling and you try to make yourself feel good, you are actually intensifying the polarity of your feelings. You are shoving the "bad" feeling down in place of trying to feel something different. Ironically, many people who struggle emotionally are, at their core, people who actually just have a greater desire to enjoy life.

STOP TRYING TO BE HAPPY

Happiness is not something you can chase. It is something you have to allow. This likely will come as a surprise to many people, as the world is so adamant about everything from positive psychology to motivational Pinterest boards. But happiness is not something you can coach yourself into.

Happiness is your natural state. That means you will return to it on your own if you allow the other feelings you want to experience to come up, be felt, be processed, and not resisted. The less you resist your unhappiness, the happier you will be. It is often just trying too hard to feel one certain way that sets us up for failure.

ARRIVE INTO THE PRESENT

There's a saying that if you're anxious, it's because you're living in the future, and if you're depressed, it's because you're living in the past. When you're living in the present moment, you realize that both the past and future are just current illusions in the infinite, eternal "now" and that they are actually ways in which you can avoid being in your body.

The only place to find happiness is in the present because that's the only place it truly exists. Trying to find happiness by focusing on what could or might happen in the future is actually a process of disassociation. Practice arriving into today by focusing on taking life one day at a time and doing the most with what you have in front of you currently.

There's a fine balance between living for the moment and taking care of your future self.

STOP TRYING TO ASSERT DOMINANCE

In his book on Hygge, the Danish art of coziness and well-being that many attribute to the nation's staggeringly high happiness rates, Meik Wiking explains that connecting with others is not just spending time with them; it has to do with not trying to dominate, impress, or create an emotional reaction in someone.[23] You find a lot more happiness by not trying to prove yourself.

People who want and need to assert their dominance in relationships are the ones who are always in arguments over hypothetical things, creating drama at important holidays or events, or otherwise finding that the very people they are supposed to love and cherish most receive the worst of their behavior.

In order to find greater happiness, you need to see yourself as an equal to those around you. When you view yourself in a position to constantly learn from all those you know, you are no longer compensating for fearing you are "beneath" them.

LEAN INTO THE LITTLE JOYS WHEN YOU FIND THEM

When we think of trying to "enjoy" life, it's common for our minds to jump to trying to achieve things that are huge, overwhelming highs. We think that being happy is only what happens when we're on vacation or just landed a huge bonus.

This, however, is actually the opposite of happiness, because it's conditional. True happiness is embracing the little joys in life: the sunrise on a warm summer morning, your cup of coffee, or an amazing book. It is being grateful not only for when big things happen, but also for the small satisfactions that you can find every day.

Most people severely overthink happiness. They assume their lives have to be in perfect working order for them to experience real joy. This is not so. Real joy is finding happiness where you are and how you are.

NURTURE POSITIVE RELATIONSHIPS WHEN YOU HAVE THEM

Regardless of whether or not you are introverted or extroverted, the quality of your relationships determines the quality of your life experiences. Tons of research backs this up: We become most like the people we spend time with, and our happiness is directly correlated with not the quantity of relationships we have, but the quality of each of them; being lonely is as much of a risk to your health as smoking.[24]

However, what most people interpret this to mean is that they should just make friends where they can find them and be close to their biological family, even if they dislike them. That's totally missing the point. Happiness is not contingent upon you forcing relationships you don't want to be in. It is, however, contingent upon you building and fostering relationships with people you really like and who add value to your life.

When you meet someone with whom you really have a connection, go out of your way to make sure you see that person and keep your friendship healthy.

LEARN SOMETHING NEW AS OFTEN AS YOU CAN

When you approach life as though you already know all there is to know, you are actually closing yourself off to potentially having new and better experiences. If you assume that you know what will happen when you try something new, or if you think you know what places you haven't been to would be like...you might just want to leave some room to surprise yourself.

Think of life as something you can constantly learn from. Your pain teaches you what does not feel good and what you should not continue to do. Your joy teaches you what is in alignment. Everything can be your teacher, and the more you allow your life experiences to shift and change you, the better you (and they) will become.

SEE CHALLENGING TIMES AS OPPORTUNITIES FOR TRANSFORMATION

Happy people aren't joyful all the time, and this is an

important distinction to make. In fact, genuinely happy people are more at peace than they are ecstatic about everything they experience.

This is because happy people are inherently coachable and changeable. They are not stuck in their ways. They understand that life requires growth, and when that growth stagnates, discomfort begins to arise.

The true nature of life is constant movement and constant evolution. If you do not keep up with that, life will all but force you to change as it becomes less and less comfortable to stay where you are. You cannot avoid all pain, but you can absolutely avoid a lot of suffering by staying focused on your internal growth.

BE AWARE OF WHAT YOU GIVE YOUR ENERGY TO

Sure, most people realize that if they work a job they dislike or stay in relationships they despise for the majority of their lives they aren't going to feel great about it. What many don't realize, however, is that there are far more significant things that we constantly offer our energy to that create the quality of our lives.

Those disliked jobs and stale relationships aren't problems, they are symptoms, and at the root of all of it is where you allow your mind to run. When you give your energy to certain thoughts, they gain life. There's a saying that the wolf that wins is the one that you feed, and when it comes to the quality of your life, you need to be extremely careful of what you allow yourself to think. It will soon become what you feel, then what you believe, and then how you behave, and sure enough, the way you live.

SCHEDULE TIME TO DO NOTHING

Happiness is an active pursuit as much as it is a passive one. Though to feel fulfilled each day is absolutely a conscious choice (it isn't going to happen by accident, FYI) the irony of really feeling good is that it's not something you can force; it's something you have to allow.

Happiness is refusing to fill your schedule to the absolute brim so you can wring the most you possibly can out of every second of your life. It is also taking time to embrace the mundanity of everyday moments. It's sitting back and reading a book, talking over dinner with someone you love, or just enjoying the small things each day. Taking this time won't happen on its own; you have to plan for it.

SCHEDULE TIME TO PLAY

When we were kids, all we did was imagine and play. Our lives were our canvases, and we inherently understood that we could make believe absolutely anything and spend the day living it out.

The same is true in adulthood, but over the course of a few decades, the world tends to have a way of beating the magic out of you. If you really want to enjoy life, you have to make time to do what you loved when you were young. Paint, play in the sand, play games you love, and be creative for the sake of it.

If that all sounds childish, good. It means you're ready to reconcile with your inner child who is and always has been there all along. Enjoying life is living it out in both the simplest and most transformative ways possible. Part of that is simply letting yourself show up and be who and how you are.

BECOMING A MASTER OF YOURSELF

When you get to the end of your life, you will begin to see your mountains for what they really were. *Gifts.*

When you look back on your life, you won't remember the hardships. You'll see them then as pivot points, growth opportunities, the days of awakening right before everything changed.

To become a master of oneself is first to take radical and complete responsibility for your life. This includes even that which is beyond your control. A true master knows that it is not what happens, but the way one responds, that determines the outcome.

Not everybody gets there. Most people live barely realizing that they are creating most of the waves in their lives and that it is also their job to learn to ride them. Most people spend their days lost in a fog of their own thoughts and feelings, having little ability to sort through them.

Mastery is to realize that we are equipped with the exact traits we need to overcome the mountains before us, and in fact, doing so is the ultimate calling of our lives. We are not only capable; we are destined.

Mastery is to finally understand that the years of discomfort you endured were not some sort of purgatory you had to just get through. They were your deepest inner self informing you that you are capable of more, deserving of better, and meant to transform into the person of your dreams.

You must claim it. You must create it. Your own healing process will create an invisible ripple effect on the collective. If we want to change the world, we change ourselves. If we want to change our lives, we change ourselves. If we want to scale the greatest mountains before us, we change how we arrive at the path.

When you reach the peak of it all—whatever that may be for you—you will look back and know that every step was worth it. More than anything, you will be overwhelmingly grateful for the pain that led you to begin your journey, because really, it wasn't trying to hurt you as much as it was trying to show you that something was wrong. That something was the risk of your potential remaining untapped, your life spent with the wrong people, doing the wrong things, and wondering why you never felt quite right.

Your life is just beginning.

One day, the mountain that was in front of you will be so far behind you, it will barely be visible in the distance. But who you become in learning to climb it? That will stay with you forever.

That is the point of the mountain.

REFERENCES

1 Halifax, Joan. *Standing at the Edge: Finding Freedom Where Fear & Courage Meet*. New York: Flatiron Books, 2018.

2 Hawking, Stephen. *A Brief History of Time*. New York: Penguin Random House, 1988.

3 Lachman, Gary. *Jung the Mystic: The Esoteric Dimensions of Carl Jung's Life and Teachings*. New York: Penguin Random House, 2010.

4 Hendricks, Gay. *The Big Leap: Conquer Your Hidden Fear and Take Life to the Next Level*. New York: HarperOne, 2009.

5 Swan, Teal. "Find Your Subconscious Core Commitment," tealswan.com.

6 Seymour, Tom. "Vagus Nerve: Function, Stimulation, And Further Research." *Medical News Today*, 2017.

7 Lieberman, Daniel Z.; Long, Michael E. *The Molecule of More: How a Single Chemical in Your Brain Drives Love, Sex, and Creativity--And Will Determine the Fate of the Human Race*. Dallas: BenBella Books, 2018.

8 Tracy, Brian. "The Role Your Subconscious Mind Plays In Your Everyday Life," briantracy.com, 2019.

9 Holiday, Ryan. "Sorry, An Epiphany Isn't What's Going To Change Your Life." ryanholiday.net, 2016.

10 Sims, Stacy T., Ph.D. "The 3 Body Types: Explained." *Runner's World*, 2016. https://www.runnersworld.com/health-injuries/a20818211/the-3-body-types-explained

11 Taylor, Christa. "Creativity and Mood Disorder: A Systematic Review and Meta-Analysis." *Perspectives on Psychological Science*, 2017.

12 Cole, Adam. "Does Your Body Really Refresh Itself Every 7 Years?" NPR, 2016. https://www.npr.org/sections/health-shots/2016/06/28/483732115/how-old-is-your-body-really

13 Bremner, J. Douglas, MD. *Traumatic Stress: Effects On The Brain.* US National Library of Medicine National Institutes of Health, 2006.

14 Burton, Neel, MD. "Our Hierarchy of Needs." *Psychology Today,* 2012. https://www.psychologytoday.com/us/blog/hide-and-seek/201205/our-hierarchy-needs

15 Jacobson, Sheri. "Inner Child Work: What Is It, And How Can You Benefit?" Harley Therapy, 2017. https://www.harleytherapy.co.uk/counselling/inner-child-work-can-benefit.htm

16 Henriques, Martha. "Can the legacy of trauma be passed down the generations?" BBC, 2019. https://www.bbc.com/future/article/20190326-what-is-epigenetics

17 Covey, Stephen. *The 7 Habits of Highly Effective People.* Mango Media, Inc. 1989.

18, 19 Hardy, Benjamin, Ph.D. "You Don't Control The Outcomes Of Your Life, Principles Do."
LinkedIn, 2017. https://www.linkedin.com/pulse/you-dont-control-outcomes-your-life-principles-do-benjamin-hardy-3

20 Lopez, Donald S. "Eightfold Path: Buddhism." *Britannica,* undated. https://www.britannica.com/topic/Eightfold-Path

21 Diamond, Stephen, Ph.D. "Essential Secrets of Psychotherapy: The Inner Child." *Psychology Today,* 2008. https://www.psychologytoday.com/us/blog/evil-deeds/200806/essential-secrets-psychotherapy-the-inner-child

22 Brenner, Gail, Ph.D. "The Warrior's Way to Inner Peace: What Is Inner Peace?" gailbrenner.com. https://gailbrenner.com/2009/11/the-warriors-way-1-inner-peace/

23 Wiking, Miek. *The Little Book of Hygge: Danish Secrets to Happy Living.* New York: HarperCollins, 2016.

24 Pomeroy, Claire. "Loneliness Is Harmful to Our Nation's Health." Scientific American, 2019. https://blogs.scientificamerican.com/observations/loneliness-is-harmful-to-our-nations-health/

BRIANNA WIEST is an author living in Pennsylvania.

briannawiest.com
instagram.com/briannawiest
facebook.com/briannawiestauthor
pinterest.com/briannawiestwords

MORE FROM BRIANNA WIEST

101 Essays That Will Change The Way You Think

This compilation of Wiest's published work features pieces on why you should pursue purpose over passion, embrace negative thinking, see the wisdom in daily routine, and become aware of the cognitive biases that are creating the way you see your life. Each will leave you thinking: this idea changed my life.

"A must-read for everyone. This seminal book literally changed the way I think and ultimately changed my life."

HELEN – GOODREADS

Salt Water: Poems On Healing & Wholeness

Salt Water is Brianna Wiest's debut poetry book which gracefully touches on the issues of self-awareness, wholeness and what it takes to reconcile with yourself.

Brianna's prose artfully illustrates how healing helps us to actualize our latent potential and bring us into a greater awe for the universe that we are so irrevocably connected to.

I Am The Hero Of My Own Life

This is the guide to getting out of your own way. *I Am the Hero of My Own Life* is a guided journal that will will help you envision your ideal life and identify the unconscious attachments that are preventing you from living it. Through a series of writing prompts and exercises, you will sort through the conflicting thoughts, feelings, and fears that are preventing you from becoming the person you want and need to be.

SAMPLE EXERCISES INCLUDE:

– Tracing your judgments of other people back to your own personal insecurities.

– Drafting a Venn diagram of your skills, your passions, and the world's needs.

– Outlining exactly the type of partner you always dreamed of marrying, then strategizing how you're going to embody those traits yourself.

– Envisioning what you'd think about and what you'd do all day if you were already healed, whole and happy.

THOUGHT CATALOG Books

THOUGHT CATALOG BOOKS is a publishing imprint of Thought Catalog, a digital magazine for thoughtful storytelling. Thought Catalog is owned by The Thought & Expression Company, an independent media group based in Brooklyn, NY, which also owns and operates Shop Catalog, a curated shopping experience featuring our best-selling books and one-of-a-kind products, and Collective World, a global creative community network. Founded in 2010, we are committed to helping people become better communicators and listeners to engender a more exciting, attentive, and imaginative world. As a publisher and media platform, we help creatives all over the world realize their artistic vision and share it in print and digital form with audiences across the globe.

Made in the USA
Coppell, TX
01 August 2021

59808861R10146